Shifting Involveme

Erekson

THE ELIOT JANEWAY LECTURES
ON HISTORICAL ECONOMICS
IN HONOR OF
JOSEPH SCHUMPETER
PRINCETON UNIVERSITY
1979

SHIFTING INVOLVEMENTS

Private Interest and Public Action

ALBERT O. HIRSCHMAN

Princeton University Press
Princeton, New Jersey

Published by Princeton University Press, 41 William Street,
Princeton, New Jersey

Library of Congress Cataloging in Publication Data will be found on
the last printed page of this book

Clothbound editions of Princeton University Press books are printed
on acid-free paper, and binding materials are chosen for strength
and durability

Printed in the United States of America by Princeton University
Press, Princeton, New Jersey

For Lara, Grégoire,
Alexander, and Nicholas

PREFACE

I am not sure that this book qualifies as a work of social science. It is so directly concerned with change and upheaval, both individual and social, that at times I had the feeling that I was writing the conceptual outline of a *Bildungsroman* (with, as always in novels, a number of autobiographical touches mixed in here and there).

This blurring of genres does not bother me, but it exacts a price. I have tried to make the various turns and transitions, which stand in the center of the essay, as compelling as possible. But they admittedly fall short of carrying the conviction and of achieving the generality which social science likes to claim for its propositions. Then again, as many of these claims have proven excessive, perhaps I need not worry.

In any event, the venture does not wholly depend on the success of my overall scheme. The journey which I undertook permitted a number of elaborate side trips which yielded, among many other observations, a critique of conventional consumption theory, a better understanding of collective action, and a new interpretation of the universal suffrage. As I came upon such byproducts, my confidence grew that the whole venture was justified, if only for its apparent heuristic value.

The invitation, in 1978, to give the Eliot Janeway Lectures in Historical Economics at Princeton University provided the initial impulse to write the present essay. One of the purposes of these lectures, which I gave in December 1979 under the title "Private and Public Happiness: Pursuits and Disappointments," is to honor the memory and intellectual heritage of Joseph Schumpeter. I believe that my inquiry into some of the discontents characteristic of our economic, social, and political order can claim to be in the Schumpeterian tradition.

Early, partial drafts of the essay were intensively discussed in seminars at the Institute for Advanced Study, at Stanford and Yale, and at the European University Institute in Florence. On and after these occasions, I have debated my points with a very large number of colleagues, orally as well as in correspondence; it would be impossible to name them all and unfair to name only a few. Some of these commentators will find themselves cited in the footnotes. Never before have I received so many excellent suggestions that just had to be incorporated, with the result that at times I felt I was turning from author into editor. Perhaps this wealth of good advice stems from the character of the book, from its coming close to being a "conceptual novel." Everyone who read the early fragments wanted the hero to behave a bit differently or had a different explanation for his or her actions. I am very grateful to all these excellent people for having thickened my plot.

Albert O. Hirschman
Princeton, New Jersey
April 1981

CONTENTS

Shifting Involvements

A Private-Public Cycle?

I started to work on this essay in June 1978 and in Paris, where a spate of articles and even books marked the tenth anniversary of the demonstrations, student uprisings, strikes, and other public actions in which large masses of citizens in Western Europe, North and South America, and Japan had participated in 1968. Many commentators noted how remote this phenomenon seemed already. Indeed, the change in mood that has taken place within so short a span of time is remarkable. An important ingredient of the "spirit of 1968" was a sudden and overwhelming concern with public issues—of war and peace, of greater equality, of participation in decision-making. This concern arose after a long period of individual economic improvement and apparent full dedication thereto on the part of large masses of people in all of the countries where these "puzzling" outbreaks occurred. While poorly understood at the time they took place, those outbreaks are today classed as abnormal and quixotic episodes; in the course of the seventies, people returned to worry primarily about their private interests, the more so as the easy forward movement that had marked the earlier period gave place almost everywhere to uncertainty and crisis. Thus, the change from the fifties to the sixties and then to the seventies and other such alternations in earlier periods raise the question whether our societies are in some way predisposed toward oscillations between periods of intense preoccupation with public issues and of almost total concentration on individual improvement and private welfare goals. In raising that question I am of course already armed with a number of arguments sug-

gesting a positive answer. But before spelling them out I wish
to stress the tentative and speculative character of the whole
undertaking. In particular, I shall be unable to *prove* the
existence of anything like what economists have traditionally
designated as cycles, that is, pendular movements of a fairly
regular duration, such as the Kitchin, Juglar, or Kondratieff
business cycles. At most, my enterprise will have something in
common with the Kondratieff cycle whose duration is so long
(50–60 years) that, given the limited historical experience with
capitalism so far, we cannot be quite sure whether it really
exists.

The construction of any theory of cycles of collective behavior must face a difficult task. To be persuasive such a theory must be endogenous: that is, one phase must be shown to
arise necessarily out of the preceding one (out of its contradictions, to use Marxian language), just as any useful business
cycle theory must be able to show how the economic down-
turn or bust follows necessarily from the preceding upswing or
boom and vice versa. If outside events like wars or spectacular
inventions can be shown to play a decisive role in making for
the periodic turning points, then the cycle is exogenously determined unless it can be shown that these events are not
really external, but can be understood as outcomes of either
upswing or downswing.

In the case of changes in collective behavior along the public-private dimension, outside events can generally be credited
with much of the responsibility. When large numbers of citizens become aroused and take part in some collective action,
the immediate reason is often found in foreign aggression, in
heightened oppression or, as Tocqueville would have it, in a
beginning of reform. Similarly, when citizens become wholly
absorbed in the pursuit of private affairs, such behavior can
usually be traced to the exceptional opportunities for economic advance opening up during that period, or, by way of
contrast, to increasing economic difficulties that compel concentration on finding a job, keeping it, and making ends meet.
Other important exogenous factors are the extent of, and
changes in, external pressures and repressions: it is easier

to participate in a public protest when one only loses time through the act of participation than when one thereby risks losing one's head.

Such outside influences and forces that *pull* people into this or that kind of behavior must obviously be part of any complete historical accounting for changes in collective behavior. They have in fact traditionally been given first or even exclusive place in such accounts. This very practice is one good reason for taking the opposite tack: that is, for calling attention to the neglected *push* factors that may lie behind the noted behavior changes. These are precisely the factors that make for a transformation of the preferences of large masses of individuals when they dwell for some time in either the private or the public sphere and then evaluate the ensuing experiences.

On occasion, a proper appreciation of such endogenous factors will substantially enrich conventional accounts of turnabouts from the private to the public sphere. An example is World War I. Modern wars are such overpowering events that they make greater attention to public affairs virtually compulsory, but their outbreak is usually explained by reference to diplomatic rivalry, economic competition, or ideological conflict, rather than to any desire on the part of citizens to be more involved in public affairs. Yet the latter explanation is not as farfetched as it sounds at first. The long period of peace and increasing prosperity which Europe experienced before the First World War produced, in important sectors of the middle and upper classes, a feeling of revulsion against bourgeois order, security, acquisitiveness, and pettiness.[1] For these groups, the war came as a release from boredom and emptiness, as a promise of the longed-for community that would transcend social class, and as an overdue return to heroic action and sacrifice. Contemporary writers such as Stefan Zweig even attempted to explain in those terms why Europe went to war in 1914.[2] This is no doubt excessive; but the accu-

---

[1] Eric J. Leed, "Class and Disillusionment in World War I," *Journal of Modern History* 50 (December 1978), 68.

[2] Leed, p. 685.

mulated disaffection from the long, peaceful, "materialist" period preceding the war does explain much about its astounding early popularity which in turn contributed to the shape the war took, to its length and intensity. In his affecting study *The Great War and Modern Memory,* Paul Fussell has graphically laid out the " 'raised,' essentially feudal language" that immediately came into widespread use in accounts of the war.[3] This language reflected an antibourgeois, proheroic ideological stance that may well bear some responsibility for the protracted and tragically murderous refusal of the generals on both sides to recognize the nonheroic realities of trench warfare.

It appears that the stress on endogenous factors in the shift of collective behavior along the private-public axis can throw new light on important turning points. In general, this essay aims at correcting the exogenous bias of previous accounts and at giving an enhanced role to people's critical appraisals of their own experiences and choices as important determinants of new and different choices. In this manner, human perception, self-perception, and interpretation should be accorded their proper weight in the unfolding of events.

A final introductory comment needs to be made on the meaning of the private-public dichotomy as used in this essay. One of the two terms offers little difficulty: *public* action, action in the *public* interest, striving for the *public* happiness—these all refer to action in the political realm, to involvement of the citizen in civic or community affairs. The antonym of public is more problematic. The ancient contrast, much debated from Aristotle down to the Renaissance, was between *vita activa,* then understood precisely as active involvement in

---

[3] New York and London: Oxford University Press, 1975, pp. 21-23. Ironically, just as the English reverted to this feudal language and embraced the war as an opportunity for knightly combat, the Germans denounced them as nothing but grubby traders and claimed heroism as their own exclusive heritage. This was the message of Werner Sombart's egregious war tract *Händler und Helden* (Leipzig: Duncker & Humblot, 1915), where the Germans were of course portrayed as the *Helden* (heroes) and the English as the despicable *Händler* (dealers, traders, shopkeepers).

public, civic affairs, and *vita contemplativa* which referred to withdrawal from the active life and studied abstention from participation in its futile struggles and excitements, for the purposes of contemplation and philosophical meditation.[4] While the contemplative life could be and has on occasion been dubbed "private," it should be clear already that it is not the kind of private life that is the subject of this essay. Rather, in a more modern vein, I distinguish here between *two varieties of active life:* one is the traditional *vita activa* which is wholly concerned with public affairs; and the other is the pursuit of a better life for oneself and one's family, "better" being understood primarily in terms of increased material welfare. This is of course today's commonsense meaning of the contrast between pursuing the public interest and attending to one's private interests.

This change in the commonly accepted antonym of action in the public interest gives a time dimension to my study. In an earlier period, "men of quality" were thought to face primarily the choice between the public life or the withdrawal therefrom for purposes of reflection. Little attention was paid to those—slaves, serfs, or simply wretched—who devoted most of their time to eking out a living. That there is a kind of very active life, engaged in also by an ever larger portion of the upper classes themselves, that is not concerned with the public good at all, but aims directly at the production and accumulation of private wealth, is strangely a rather recent discovery. It was made slowly with the rise of commerce and industry in the seventeenth and eighteenth centuries, and only in the early nineteenth century was it explicitly incorporated into political thought by Benjamin Constant (see Chapter 6). Closely related is the emergence, in the same period, of the idea that the pursuit of one's private, material *interests* is a wholly legitimate form of human conduct, one that may in fact be preferable, *from the point of view of society,* to a life of intensive involvement with public affairs. For this life was

[4] Hannah Arendt's *The Human Condition* (Chicago: University of Chicago Press, 1958) starts with a wide-ranging discussion of *vita activa* and *vita contemplativa.*

now seen as a privileged arena for the more dangerous *passions* of men, such as ambition, envy, and the reckless pursuit of glory and power.

The private-public dichotomy, theme of the present book, has therefore much in common with that of my recent essay in intellectual history, *The Passions and the Interests* (Princeton University Press, 1977). But I proceed here in a very different way. While I go from time to time on excursions into political and intellectual history, my main purpose is not historical: rather, I attempt a *phenomenology* of involvements and disappointments that is meant to account for the swings from private concerns to public action and back. In the nature of such an enterprise, the present study does not evolve within a specific historical time; instead it aims at describing the general features of processes that take place recurrently over a prolonged period. Nevertheless, the observations that have just been made about the emergence of the private-public dichotomy as understood here supply a historical time frame: it is only since pursuit of private interests has been widely and explicitly recognized as a serious rival to involvement in public affairs that the private-public cycle which is to be described here can claim to exist at all.

CHAPTER 1

On Disappointment

The Role of Disappointment
in Preference Change

As just presented, my topic can be considered a special case of a more general problem: how to account for preference change, not just from private-oriented to public-oriented activity and vice versa, but quite generally from commodity A to commodity B or from activity A to activity B. Since change in tastes or preferences is an undeniable fact of considerable importance, particularly in Western societies, one might expect a sizable literature to have accumulated on the topic. Actually, at least insofar as economics is concerned, this expectation is largely contradicted. The reason is that economic analysis proceeds on the basis of preferences that are considered to be given (even though they may occasionally be changing) as a result of physiological needs and psychological and cultural propensities. Any number of quotations from economists and economics textbooks could be supplied to the effect that economics had no business delving into the reasons why preferences are what they are, and it is implicit in such denials that it is even less appropriate for economists to inquire how and why preferences might change.

Such assertions about the proper province of "scientific, positive," economics are often made in so annoyed a tone and so aggressive a manner that one may well suspect here some basic sensitivity and vulnerability. Indeed, the critics of orthodoxy have long made the alleged givenness of tastes and preferences into one of the principal targets of their attack on the neoclassical edifice. The concept of "consumer sovereignty" with its implication that consumers have independently acquired tastes and can make producers conform to their wishes by the way in which they "vote" their dollars in the market-place has been held up to considerable ridicule by John Kenneth Galbraith and others who stress the way in which consumer tastes are molded by the production decisions and advertising of large corporations.

Moreover, economists not particularly hostile to the whole structure of neoclassical analysis, but simply dissatisfied with the peculiar agnosticism of their discipline in an important area, have lately begun to build changes of tastes into their models of consumer and market behavior.[1] Indeed, one prominent economist, Tibor Scitovsky, has made an original and stimulating attempt, by drawing on modern psychology, to refine our understanding of the nature and constituents of consumer satisfaction. In the process he has made a considerable contribution to the topic of preference-formation.[2]

The approach I wish to propose here differs substantially from most of these writings, and for that reason I shall set it forth in a straightforward fashion, with only a few references to work, such as Scitovsky's, that is related to mine in important ways.

My basic point is easily stated: acts of consumption, as well as acts of participation in public affairs, which are undertaken because they are expected to yield satisfaction, also yield disappointment and dissatisfaction. They do so for different reasons, in different ways, and to different degrees, but to the extent that the disappointment is not wholly eliminated by an instantaneous downward adjustment of expectations, any pattern of consumption or of time use carries within itself, to use the hallowed metaphor, "the seeds of its own destruction."

[1] See, in particular, Carl Christian von Weizsäcker, "Notes on Endogenous Change of Tastes," *Journal of Economic Theory* 3 (1971), 345–372, and the papers presented by Robert A. Pollak, Edgar A. Pessemier, and T. A. Marschak at a session on "Changes in Consumer Preferences" at the 90th Annual Meeting of the American Economic Association, reprinted in *American Economic Review* 68 (May 1978), 374–391.

[2] *The Joyless Economy* (New York: Oxford University Press, 1976).

It is easy to see, even at this initial stage of the argument, how this general proposition could yield an explanation of systematic changes in consumer behavior and citizen activities.

My task is to demonstrate the strength of the basic proposition I have just laid out. But then, is that really necessary? Don't we all know, intinctively and intuitively, as well as from the writings of poets and philosophers, that disappointment and discontent are eternally the human lot, regardless of achievements, be they distinction, wealth, or power? Later I shall return to the idea that humans, in contrast to animals, are never satisfied, that it is their very nature to be intrinsically unsatisfiable, insatiable. Now I shall just cite a most concise statement to this effect which Kant is reported to have made in conversation with the Russian historian Karamzin: "Give a man everything he desires and yet at this very moment he will feel that this *everything* is not *everything*."[3] An implicit comparison is made here with satisfiable creatures, and it demonstrates that, even at the limit, disappointment is a central element of the human experience. This so-called characteristic of human nature has often been related to the mortality of man and to human consciousness of this mortality; it also has been the starting point for discussions about the existence of God.

Three remarks are in order. First, it is well to be aware of this human-nature dimension of our concept: even though this dimension will be excluded from much of the discussion, it cannot help but lurk somewhere in the background. Second, a look at the intellectual history around the topic will probably reveal that the stress on the "insatiable," "eternally dissatisfied" aspect of human nature is characteristic of a *certain phase* of *Western* civilization and could therefore tell us something quite useful about the particular strength and pervasiveness of feelings of disappointment with material wealth at a certain place and time in history (see Chapter 3). Third, an

---

[3] Cited from N. M. Karamzin, *Letters of a Russian Traveller, 1789-1790* (New York, 1957), pp. 40–41 in Joseph Frank, *Dostoevsky, The Seeds of Revolt, 1821-1849* (Princeton: Princeton University Press, 1976), p. 57; italics in the text.

attempt will be made here *not* to appeal to human nature in explaining disappointment, but to relate it to specific aspects of economic structure and development. If economists have disregarded the phenomenon, this may be precisely because they thought it had *only* a metaphysical or "human nature" aspect which is safe to neglect because it would affect all human consumption activities equally, leading to a uniform "discount," as it were, on all satisfactions. The tendency to be disappointed could then be considered as an unfortunate and perverse quirk of human nature, one that really ought not to be there if only man were a more "rational actor." Provided basic needs are taken care of, and welfare, as measured by consumption and leisure, is on the increase, people ought to feel better off—if they are not, so much the worse for them: the economist will deem them to *be* better off!

It is thus possible that the general human disposition to be disappointed has hidden from view the fact that there are important *variations* in the incidence and intensity of disappointment at different times and in relation to different activities and commodities. In any event, I shall here take a leaf from an ancient book and deal with people the way they really are rather than the way some authorities (in this case the economists) think they ought to behave. To make progress with such an inquiry, I shall first call attention to some elementary characteristics of human consumption which, strangely, seem to have escaped scrutiny.

Before actually engaging in any activity, including that of consumption, people formulate the *project* to do so. Part of this project are certain mental images or *expectations* about its nature and about the kind and degree of satisfaction it will yield. The independent existence of the project with its expectations implies that it may differ considerably from reality as it is experienced when the project is executed, that is, when consumption actually takes place. Hence the possibility of either disappointment or, perhaps, of its opposite. Not much attention will be paid to the latter case simply because it seems to happen so infrequently, in comparison with the former. This bias of our inquiry finds some justification in a similar bias of language: there is no *single* word in any language, so it seems, for the antonym of disappointment—one must make do with a circumlocution such as "pleasant surprise."[4] The reason is probably that it is much more common for expectations to exceed reality than for reality to exceed expectations. The point is strengthened if one looks at the German word for disappointment, *Enttäuschung* ("dis-deception"). Here the general meaning of expectations-gone-wrong has been swamped by one of its varieties: the word literally means unmaking or unraveling of an error or mistake in judgment and might therefore be expected to refer to any conceivable kind of mistaken expectations; but it has taken on the specific meaning of disappointment, presumably because the mistakes that are in fact committed most of the time are those of expecting too much from reality.[5] Be it noted that, when it is a matter of actual experience rather than expectations, language has no similar pessimistic bias: there are many terms—happiness, joy, bliss, and so on—denoting pleasurable experiences as such. This makes the asymmetry of language with respect to the confrontations of expectation and experience still more significant.

[4] Economists have used the term "windfall" or "windfall profits" to denote unanticipated gains. But the term denotes the *fact* of realizing higher-than-expected profits rather than the *feelings* connected with that event. Also, the term is untranslatable into other languages—one simply renders it as unanticipated profits.

[5] Moreover, there are several terms with meanings close to disappointment, such as disillusion and disenchantment, and they suggest that the hopeful expectations that were entertained were an illusion from the start. The idea here seems to be that any hopeful expectation always contains an element of illusion, so by its very nature reality can never quite come up to it, let alone exceed it. This thought is carried to its ultimate conclusion in certain usages of Spanish (for example, in Argentina) were *ilusión* is used interchangeably with *esperanza* (hope). In French, the terms *décevoir* and *déception* were equivalent to the English "to deceive" and "deception" (in line with the Latin *decipere*) until the sixteenth century and then slowly assumed the present-day meaning "to disappoint" and "disappointment." This evolution of meaning testifies to an important truth: the quintessential deception to which humans are subject is that of the hopes they themselves fabricate.

Taking Disappointment Seriously

A number of changes in collective behavior become more intelligible if the concept of disappointment is given its due. The persuasiveness of this contention will be tested in the subsequent chapters, which will explore the varieties of disappointment with the alternating pursuits of private and public happiness. But before embarking on this journey some general issues arising out of my chosen theme must be discussed.

Consider first a methodological objection to the prospective study. The argument of this book will be largely in terms of the experience of the individual consumer-citizen or at best of the individual household. As a result, there arises the familiar micro-macro problem. Supposing a convincing case is made for a private-public-private cycle (due to successive disappointments) in the case of an individual, what does this mean at the societal level? Not necessarily all that much: aggregate disappointment with private consumption activities (or with public endeavors) could be roughly constant through time as successive consumer-citizen groups are in turn victims of disappointment. This would be the case, for example, if disappointment were exclusively related to age and the life cycle *and* if there were no baby booms or subsequent declines in birth rate.[6] But aggregate disappointment could vary over time if certain new consumption experiences with a higher-than-average disappointment potential were lived through at the same time by important social groups. These are the processes I shall focus on primarily as I attempt to understand why large groups of people will on occasion move together from the pursuit of one kind of happiness to that of another. I shall therefore pay particular attention to structural changes in mass consumption that occur in the course of economic growth and development and that may be accompanied by

---

[6] For cycles in optimism and pessimism generated by demographic waves of this sort, see Richard Easterlin, *Birth and Fortune: The Impact of Numbers on Personal Welfare* (New York: Basic Books, 1980).

the outcropping of the more solid variety of disappointment which will be discussed shortly.

In a sense, the approach raises questions about the existence of genuine private-public cycles. A cycle is presumably defined as a process in whose course identical forces are responsible over and over again for moving economy or society from one phase to the next. But if the disappointment-generating forces are largely tied up with a specific and therefore nonrecurrent phase of the historical growth process, then there can be no assurance that such forces will ever emerge again. Nonetheless, somewhat similar movements of disappointment or revulsion have surfaced repeatedly in the course of capitalist development even though the specific consumption experiences that gave rise to these movements were different each time. I shall look at this strange backlash and speculate about some reasons for it further on, in Chapter 3.

Moreover, there is no denying that certain external events (wars, revolutions, etc.) do play an important role in suddenly and substantially raising the degree of participation in public affairs. As was argued in the Introduction, such events may in part be caused by the disappointments of the previous private phase, but once they take place they draw in all kinds of people and thus compel a synchronization of public concerns and therefore of the public-private cycle. The same is true for periods of rapid economic growth—such growth similarly induces large groups of people to concentrate for a while on their private affairs, with the result that they will go together through any disappointment experiences that may unfold during that phase.[7]

Next I shall deal with two objections against the proposed emphasis on disappointment as a driving force in human affairs. The first derives from the psychological theory of cognitive dissonance. According to this theory, people who have made a purchase or a commitment will go to considerable lengths, for the sake of peace of mind and "cognitive consis-

---

[7] A further remark on the micro-macro problem is on p. 93.

tency," in *suppressing* evidence and information tending to show that they may have made a mistake and are in for disappointment. In one of the earliest and best known applications of the theory, automobile buyers are found to read a variety of car ads *prior* to their purchase, but once they have selected, say, a Chevrolet they will concentrate on Chevrolet ads. They thereby seek confirmation of their good judgment and avoid "dissonant" information. This is a quite interesting finding, no doubt, even though in historical perspective it appears to be conditioned a bit by the conformism of the fifties, the decade in which the theory was worked out.[8] But its intention could not possibly have been to abrogate disappointment, to deny its existence or importance as a human experience. Surely, the Chevrolet buyer whose car develops a crack in the cylinder block, so that white smoke is pouring out of the tail pipe,[9] is unlikely to react to this mishap by stepping up the rate at which he reads Chevrolet ads! There are then obviously limits to the sort of self-deception that is posited by cognitive dissonance theory.

The findings of the theory can in fact be reinterpreted: the denial of reality that is practiced testifies to the *power* and *vitality* of the disappointment experience. We engage in all kinds of ingenious ruses and delaying actions before admitting to ourselves that we *are* disappointed, in part surely because we know that disappointment may compel us to a painful reassessment of our preferences and priorities. At the same time, knowledge of these psychological processes permits an understanding of the likely shape of the disappointment experience. Disappointment frequently will have to pass a certain threshold before it is consciously avowed—but then, just be-

[8] Leon Festinger's work, *A Theory of Cognitive Dissonance,* was published by Stanford University Press in 1957; some of his basic papers were published several years earlier.

[9] As vividly chronicled in Penny Addiss, "The Life History Complaint Case of Martha and George Rose: 'Honoring the Warranty' " in Laura Nader, ed., *No Access to Law: Alternatives to the American Judicial System* (New York: Academic Press, 1980), pp. 171–189.

cause of the earlier delaying actions, it may well be experienced "with a vengeance."[10]

The second objection to giving so much importance to the concept of disappointment arises out of the economist's usual assumptions about rational behavior and learning. One reason that economists have not worried about the disappointment potential of various consumption experiences is the classical assumption of perfect knowledge. In accordance with this postulate, people are supposed to calibrate their purchases and time uses by matching their preferences, which are fully known to them, against the equally well-known world of available consumption experiences. Under these unreal circumstances, the idea that you may find out about your *real* preferences in the act of consumption, and that you may change your previous preferences as a result, is excluded almost by definition. Taking advantage of some early suggestions by Herbert Simon and Charles E. Lindblom, general decision theory has become more sophisticated in the last two or three decades by incorporating uncertainty, ignorance, and complexity; more specifically, a number of writers have acknowledged that decision-makers will change both their probabilities *and* their utilities as a result of information acquired through their own actions and experiences.[11] But the models deriving from such ideas have remained at a high level of abstraction and have not been applied to consumption theory.

It so happens that one important group of consumer purchases is rather well modeled by the classical, unsophisticated assumption of perfect knowledge. Much of consumption is typically repetitive, hence both tastes and the goods to satisfy them are well known to the consumer. As a result, gaps be-

---

[10] For a similar critique of cognitive dissonance theory, see my *Exit, Voice, and Loyalty* (Cambridge, Mass.: Harvard University Press, 1970), pp. 92–95 and Appendix E.

[11] See, for example, Richard M. Cyert and Morris H. De Groot, "Adaptive Utility" in R. H. Day and T. Groves, eds., *Adaptive Economic Models* (New York: Academic Press, 1975), pp. 223–246.

tween expectations and experience are in fact quite small and consumers continuously and rapidly can close any such gaps by lowering expectations, shifting purchases the next time around, or both. This observation yields a first typology in that it immediately reveals that the potential for lasting and serious disappointment varies considerably from one kind of purchase to another: learning from, and reacting to, previous disappointment is easy, rapid, and leads to only marginal rearrangements of consumption when the purchase is frequently repeated. Examples are food and other nondurable, everyday items whose value is small relative to income. In the case of such purchases, any disappointment experience is rapidly incorporated into the consumer's comparative appraisal of different commodities, and the gap between expectations and experience never stays open for long. Under these conditions disappointment could be smoothly self-liquidating. Matters are quite different for goods that are durable, unique, and/or whose value is large in relation to income so that their purchase cannot or need not be repeated frequently (or ever, in the case of truly unique goods). In the case of durables, moreover, their continued "hanging around" serves as a nagging reminder of any disappointment they may have occasioned. Under such circumstances, disappointment will be comparatively solid, that is, not easily liquidated; it will also be arresting to those experiencing it, could come to lead an independent existence and affect the social and cultural climate. Most important, it is likely to produce changes in consumption and activities patterns that are anything but marginal.

I shall deal here primarily with such comparatively solid disappointment. Borrowing from the language of ecology and pollution, one might call it "nonbiodegradable." In view of the nature of the goods and services involved, the nonbiodegradable variety of disappointment will be encountered mostly in wealthier societies and particularly in societies where a substantial demand for such items appears for the first time, that is, where the transition to greater wealth occurs. Examples will be supplied in the next chapter. But even in the case of ordinary, repetitive consumption experiences, where the response to disappointments takes the form either of an immediate shifting to other varieties or of the scaling down of expectations next time around, the adjustment is not as smooth as it may sound. The shifting to other varieties causes search costs, and the scaling down of expectations is not costless either: its necessity is itself felt as a loss and a disappointment.

The idea that consumers are able to calibrate their purchases in such a manner as to approach asymptotically, for each item, the optimal amount to be purchased is therefore generally off the mark, more so of course for some items than for others. Consumer overbuying and the disappointment consequent upon it are very much part of the "tâtonnement" of market processes which resemble, more than we like to admit, the general human experience which William Blake had in mind when he wrote: "You never know what is enough unless you know what is more than enough."[12]

Having defended myself against possible objections to the importance I am attributing to the experience of disappointment, I am ready to go over to the offensive. Armed with the model of a consumer-citizen who experiences systematic preference shifts in response to distinctive waves of disappointments, I can question the realism not only of the economic analysis of consumer satisfaction but also of the broader sociological views on the constituent elements of human happiness.

Take first the well-known economic analysis of the consumer: here individuals have a variety of needs and wants among which they make choices and tradeoffs so as to arrive at some optimal position at given market prices and income/leisure preferences. Economists recognize, of course, that some highly valued pursuits, such as the cultivation of friends and family ties, participation in public affairs, etc., carry no explicit price tag, but this complication is curtly dismissed by the observation that all these pursuits take time and

---

[12] William Blake, *The Marriage of Heaven and Hell*, plate 9, line 7.

therefore carry implicit price tags in terms of income (and time-consuming consumption activities) foregone.[13]

Other social scientists have criticized this manner of modeling man's search for satisfaction and happiness. First of all, they accuse the economist of making the tail wag the dog by extending to all other human activities an analysis that is appropriate to the market. They point to research showing that "commodities themselves, and the income to purchase them, are only weakly related to the things that make people happy: autonomy, self-esteem, family felicity, tension-free leisure, friendship."[14] Second, monetary and nonmonetary wants are not only difficult to compare, but social arrangements often have the specific effect and probable purpose of making sure that such activities as worship, mourning, family visits, participation in public affairs (through voting or otherwise) are *not* compared with income-producing or consumption activities—most of the nonmonetary activities just listed are construed as duties for precisely that reason. In other words, a good portion of our social arrangements is meant to *prevent* that equalization-at-the-margin of the satisfactions derived from our various activities which is the crux of the economic model.

From my point of view, this critique, interesting and pertinent though it is, does not go far enough. It still proceeds from the premise of a comprehensive range of wants, all crying out for simultaneous satisfaction. To their credit, psychologists and sociologists have been much more interested than econo-

---

[13] The observation that all activity takes scarce time is crucial to the claim that all human pursuits come within the purview of neoclassical economic analysis. In this sense, Gary Becker's analysis of time as a limited good, "A Theory of the Allocation of Time," *Economic Journal* 75 (Sept. 1965), 493–517, is the foundation stone for his enterprise of apprehending the most varied aspects of human behavior "from the economic point of view."

[14] Robert E. Lane, "Markets and the Satisfaction of Human Wants," *Journal of Economic Issues* 12 (December 1978), 815. The present paragraph is largely based on this excellent paper, which is also rich in footnote references to the sociological and psychological literature on want satisfaction.

mists in the actual makeup of human wants, that is, in the basic constituents of "happiness." Here the general procedure has been to survey the social scene and human behavior through observation and introspection and to draw up some plausible list and hierarchy of wants that make some important contribution to the feeling of well-being, from food to friendship and the feeling of intrinsic worth, from "having" to "being." An enormous amount of research into the constituents of happiness has been conducted along these lines, particularly since sociologists discovered that it is possible to *ask* people whether they are happy (and more happy now than last year, etc.) and to relate such findings not only to income but also to a number of other variables, such as, precisely, autonomy, self-esteem, and so on.

The trouble with such studies is that they are still too close to the original assumption of the economist that the consumer carries within himself a universe of wants of known intensity that he matches against prices. Both the economist and the happiness-researching sociologist think in terms of individuals pursuing an array of fixed goals or operating in terms of a set of values known to them. Now this seems to me a mistaken view of the way men and women behave. *The world I am trying to understand in this essay is one in which men think they want one thing and then upon getting it, find out to their dismay that they don't want it nearly as much as they thought or don't want it at all and that something else, of which they were hardly aware, is what they really want.* We never operate in terms of a comprehensive hierarchy of wants established by some psychologist surveying the multifarious pursuits and "needs" of mankind, but at any one point in our real existence—and that is often true also for whole societies—we pursue *some* goals which then get replaced by others.

This is the process I shall try to make intelligible here. I recognize it as an important limitation of the present study that I am dealing only with the shift from private consumption goals to action in the public interest and back again. There surely are other shifts, such as those from income maximization to the search for a different variety of private happiness through the cultivation of family and friends or through other forms of a "post-materialist" life-style.[15] But I have two arguments justifying the decision to limit myself to the private-public-private cycle. First, a beginning had to be made somewhere; the task I had set myself was so novel and arduous that I could not aspire to breaking ground everywhere at once. Second, and more important, the occasional movement of large numbers of people into the public arena tends to have such momentous historical consequences that this particular shift, even though it may be undertaken only by a small fraction of a country's total population, is of particular interest for the understanding of social change.

A final remark. The concept of disappointment cannot be given its due unless we appeal to some of the more philosophical matters that, as I said before, cannot but lurk in the background of my topic. The tendency to consider disappointment a mere temporary irritant on the way to an optimal solution on the part of a consumer who is constantly learning will not be wholly overcome until it is realized that the elimination of disappointment, the prompt closing of any gap between expectations and reality, should not be accepted without question as either feasible or desirable.

The argument on feasibility (or rather nonfeasibility) is simple. As I have suggested before, human societies have a peculiarly wide latitude for deterioration because of one of their characteristic achievements: the surplus above subsistence.[16] Once this proposition is extended from the social to the individual level, a fresh meaning can be given to the rather tired saying *errare humanum est* or "To err is human." Ordinarily understood as an invitation to forbearance for an occasional mistake, the saying can be totally reinterpreted to mean that mistake-making is an exclusive *faculty* of humans. In

---

[15] For data on the emergence of such a life-style in the Western democracies, see Ronald Inglehart, *The Silent Revolution: Changing Values and Political Styles among Western Publics* (Princeton: Princeton University Press, 1977).

[16] *Exit, Voice, and Loyalty,* pp. 6–7.

other words, the meaning of the saying is not "to err is only human," but "only humans err." In all of creation, only man is *empowered* to make mistakes and every once in a while he or she does use this power to the fullest. Lichtenberg, the eighteenth-century German scientist and aphorist, pointed to this meaning when he wrote: "To make mistakes is also *human* in the sense that animals make few mistakes or none at all, with the possible exception of the most intelligent among them."[17] If it is accepted that mistake-making is the inevitable counterpart of the very rise of man above subsistence and animal existence, then another inevitability follows: that of regret and disappointment resulting from the errors of one's ways which were surely paved not only with good intentions, but with high expectations *not* to make mistakes. So much for the possibility of ever conquering disappointment. But supposing even it were possible, would the elimination of disappointment be desirable?

While a life filled with disappointment is a sad affair, a life without any disappointment may not be bearable at all. For disappointment is the natural counterpart of man's propensity to entertain magnificent vistas and aspirations. Is this propensity unfortunate and irrational? Given the certainty of death (for one thing), what would life be without the ever renewed production of such disappointment-yielding expectations and aspirations? In other words, the "cost" of disappointments may well be less than the "benefit" yielded by man's ability to entertain over and over again the idea of bliss and happiness, disappointment-bound though it may be. As a friend of Don Quixote exclaims after the Knight of the Mournful Countenance has been cured of his madness, close to the end of his life:

[17] Georg Christoph Lichtenberg, *Aphorismen, Schriften, Briefe* (Munich: Hanser, 1974), p. 139. Similarly, C. S. Peirce is reported to have believed that "the most distinctive fact about men's lives was the existence of their errors." See R. Jackson Wilson, *In Quest of Community: Social Philosophy in the United States, 1860–1920* (New York: Wiley, 1968), pp. 47–48.

God forgive you for the damage you have caused everyone in wishing to return to sanity this most amusing fool! Don't you realize, Sir, that the benefit that might accrue from the sanity of Don Quixote will never come up to the pleasure he gives us through his follies?[18]

It is this sort of benefit-cost calculus that would be very much in order if ever disappointment were successfully gotten rid of.

[18] Book 2, Chapter 65.

CHAPTER 2

Varieties of
Consumer Disappointment

Disappointment is so common and therefore so seemingly transparent an experience that no one appears to have bothered to explore its nature, components, and varieties in systematic fashion. My principal concern in this chapter is with disappointments incidental to the private consumption of goods and services. These are obviously not the only possible disappointments with one's private pursuits. A very important category of disappointment has to do with the job experience. One reason why it is not dealt with here is the existence of a large literature on job satisfaction and dissatisfaction in which economists have begun to take an active part.[1] Another is my suspicion that one potent reason for job dissatisfaction could be tied up not so much, as is generally assumed, with the characteristics of the job as with the general satisfaction workers experience as members of society and therefore also as consumers. Because jobs in our society are primarily considered as a means to the earning of income which in turn serves to pay for consumption, the quality of the consumption experience—or the quality of life experience in general—could easily reflect on the quality of the job experience. This is in fact the conclusion reached in a recent study of the apparent drop in job satisfaction that took place in the course of the seventies in the United States. Having unsuccessfully tested explanations that relate the drop to various job characteristics, the author concludes: "... the recent decline in job satisfaction ... may have very little to do with jobs or conditions of employ-

---

[1] See the papers on "Quality of Working Life," by Karl-Olof Faxém, Richard B. Freeman, and Lester C. Thurow, in *American Economic Review* 68 (May 1978), 131–148, and Graham L. Staines, "Is Worker Dissatisfaction Rising?" *Challenge* 2 (May/June 1979), 38–45.

ment at all. We may instead be witnessing a much broader
social malaise. . . ."[2]

Without necessarily subscribing to this thesis, I shall focus
here on the world of objects and consumption expenditures as
possible and differential sources of disappointment and discontent. The idea that some goods may have more disappointment potential than others is present, albeit at a very
high level of aggregation, in a brilliant passage of Georg Simmel's *Philosophy of Money* (1900). Simmel distinguishes between money, on the one hand, and all consumer goods, on
the other, and notes that, insofar as money is desired purely
for the purpose of accumulation (by the avaricious, for example), its possession is immune to disappointment.[3] The reason
for this is the abstract character of money which is "a thing
absolutely devoid of quality" and therefore totally known: a
dollar is a dollar is a dollar, far more so than a rose is a rose is
a rose. Here is the principal psychological difference between
money and other goods which all are paradoxically *richer*
than money as they "harbor either surprises or disappointments" that are experienced in the course of use.[4]

In the present chapter, I shall attempt to carry forward the
inquiry pioneered by Simmel and look at some reasons why,
within the universe of goods, the disappointment potential of

[2] Staines, "Worker Dissatisfaction," p. 44.

[3] *Philosophie des Geldes* (Leipzig: Duncker & Humblot, 1907, 2nd ed.),
pp. 246–249. See also my comment on this passage in *Passions and Interests,* pp. 55–56.

[4] From the context of this passage it is clear that Simmel was thinking
almost exclusively in terms of *disappointments:* in the immediately preceding pages he talks at length about the "terrible discrepancy between
desire and fulfillment" and again about the "often tragic, often comical
incommensurability between desire and fulfillment." Another point: my
earlier semantic observation (see p. 13) is confirmed by the passage
quoted in the text; Simmel made here an attempt to be evenhanded as
between disappointment and its opposite, but language did not collabo-
rate since it does not have a compact term for the antonym of disappointment. Hence, Simmel is awkwardly reduced to using "surprise"
(*Überraschung*), which is a strictly neutral term—a surprise can be either
pleasant or unpleasant—as the opposite of the negative-valued "disappointment" (*Enttäuschung*).

some categories of goods might be greater than that of others. My method will be inductive rather than deductive: I start with some well-established subdivisions among consumer purchases, such as durables vs. nondurables, or goods vs. services, and then inquire whether there inheres in some of these subcategories a characteristic that makes for particularly high (or low) propensity to disappointment. Once the characteristics that make for low or high propensity to disappointment have been identified, they are of course likely to define sets of goods that do not precisely overlap with the simple-minded, given categories that have been fashioned for quite different purposes. A good example of this procedure follows immediately.

The Privileged Position of Truly Nondurable Goods

In this section as well as in the next, I shall draw on some of the conceptual distinctions, taken from psychology, which Tibor Scitovsky has recently proposed to explain why our economy is "joyless." His point of departure is the notion of *arousal* of the nervous system: when arousal is too high, the result is *discomfort* in the form of hunger, thirst, or physical pain; and when it is too low, boredom—another, peculiarly human, kind of discomfort—sets in. When either of these two varieties of discomfort is relieved by various consumption activities designed to satisfy wants or to relieve boredom, the result is both *pleasure* and *comfort:* pleasure is the experience of traveling from discomfort to comfort while the latter is achieved at the point of arrival. Hence a contradiction between pleasure and comfort: for pleasure to be experienced, comfort must be sacrificed temporarily.

While contrasting comfort with pleasure in this manner, Scitovsky chooses largely to ignore the pleasures that have their origin in various drives (food, sex, sleep), and in the ensuing satisfaction of primary wants; he concentrates instead on those pleasures that come from keeping boredom at bay, on what he calls "stimulation."[5] His reason is that, in the affluent societies with which he is primarily concerned, want satisfaction may be taken for granted and is crowded out as a source of pleasure by stimulation. This focus on stimulation and on the different extent to which it is practiced through various devices by consumers in different affluent societies is central to Scitovsky's assertion that consumers in the United States suffer from understimulation in comparison to Western Europeans. However that may be, it seems a pity that he has almost wholly neglected the very considerable portion of our pleasures that still derive, no matter how affluent we may be, from catering to our physiological needs. As these needs are recurrent, comfort gives way automatically to discomfort with the passage of time so that the pleasure-yielding trip back to comfort can once again be undertaken. We are dealing here with truly paradigmatic pleasures—simple, familiar, yet intense and indefinitely renewable as long as we live. A closer look at the goods supplying these pleasures is useful as a first step toward evaluating the comparative disappointment potential of various consumer purchases.

We all know the adage: "The best things in life are free." Let me now propose the following, only slightly more complex variant: "Some of the most durable (that is, renewable) and least disappointment-prone pleasures in life are those to be gotten from nondurable goods that are literally *consumed,* that vanish in the act of consumption." The division of the universe of consumer goods that is implicit in this statement is somewhat different from the usual one between durables and nondurables. The latter category conventionally contains such items as clothing and shoes. But from the point of view of pleasure generation and disappointment potential, the important distinction is between the *truly* nondurable goods, primarily food and fuel, that must be used up to the greatest possible extent (i.e., except for waste products of which ideally there should be none) in the process of consumption, and all those goods where decay and impairment resulting from use

[5] *Joyless Economy,* p. 79.

or the passage of time are accepted only as inevitable imperfections. Food has a special ability to provide pleasure that is based on the body's recurring physiological need for the energy it supplies. Foodstuffs disappear precisely in the process of conveying their energy to the body, and their disappearance is essential to the pleasure felt in the act of consumption.[6] That disappearance also makes for the privileged position the truly nondurable commodities hold with regard to the potential for disappointment: they are very different from the more durable goods, also known as "possessions," that are still there after disappointment has been experienced in the process of consumption and act thereby as reminders of such disappointments. Moreover, at the inevitable subsequent moments of discouragement and unhappiness, the "possessions" may well *compound* those feelings: we realize resentfully that these possessions have failed to bring the hoped-for private happiness, or experience self-reproach for feeling terrible when we should feel great, considering all these goods at our command.

There is then something both pleasure-intensive and peculiarly disappointment-resistant about goods that disappear in the process of consumption. The Roman emperors knew, so it seems, what they were doing when they took care to supply the masses with bread and circuses: *both* vanish once you have taken them in, without leaving behind a corporeal shape on which consumers can vent any disappointment, boredom, or anxiety they may have suffered or may yet suffer.

[6] In the twenties a Nobel-prize winning British chemist, Frederick Soddy, published a book, *Wealth, Virtual Wealth and Debt* (New York: Dutton, 1933, 2nd ed.), that caused a certain stir and went through several editions. The book is quite forgotten today and, on the whole, for good reasons. But on pp. 116–18 the author makes an interesting point which I amplify here for my own purposes: some basic goods, such as food and fuel, have the function to release energy for the use of humans and they *must* change, deteriorate, or perish in the performance of this function—this characteristic sets them off from all other consumer goods which are ideally unchanging. Annette Weiner who called my attention to the book also cites this point in her paper "More Desired than Gold: A Study of Women, Their Wealth and Political Evolution in the Pacific," unpublished, 1981.

It is necessary to point out and to stress the privileged position, from our point of view, of those truly nondurable goods, for language is not at all cooperative in this endeavor: durable seems offhand so much preferable to nondurable and perishable. The Greeks invented the Midas myth to remind themselves that durability has a few drawbacks, but somehow the lesson has not sunk in. Language has no generic term with a positive connotation for those goods whose outstanding merits are wholly bound up with their *non*durability.[7] Moreover, the low esteem in which perishable goods are held has been compounded, at least insofar as economists are concerned, by the well-known fact that income elasticity of demand for these goods is lower than for durables (and services). As a result, the important compensating virtues of our truly nondurables, the sturdiness of the pleasures purveyed by them and their resistance to disappointment, have been lost from view.

In extolling the truly nondurable goods as particularly disappointment-resistant I certainly do not wish to affirm that they are disappointment-*exempt*. They cannot wholly overcome that human incapacity for achieving fulfillment which was so well characterized by Kant (see page 11). Actually, this incapacity was frequently illustrated in the age of Kant by reference to the very experience of eating and drinking: Edward Young in his enormously successful *Night Thoughts,* Samuel Johnson in *Rasselas* and Giacomo Leopardi in one of his major poems, all compare the total contentment sheep feel after grazing to the lingering dissatisfaction and *ennui* that is (so they allege) the lot of the shepherd after he has had *his*

---

[7] One reason may be that foodstuffs dominate the category of truly nondurable goods. Yet, there are others: fuel, soap, cosmetics, and pharmaceuticals, to cite just a few of some importance. A second reason is the modern alteration in the meaning of the term consumption. Originally we *consumed* turnips and candles whereas we *owned* and *used* gowns and carriages, but with time (and the progress of macroeconomics) consumption came to refer to *all* the goods and services people produced or purchased for their own use. "Consumables" would once have been an apt and reasonably positive term for the category of goods I have in mind, but it has by now been contaminated by the diluted meaning of consumption.

meal.[8] But the fact that eating is here singled out as being subject to disappointment, far from contradicting my thesis, rather serves to confirm it: to make their point about the basic, metaphysical incapacity of man to achieve happiness and fulfillment in the strongest possible terms, these writers focused on those human consumption activities that are comparatively least subject to disappointment. If even eating and drinking, so they argue implicitly, are followed by feelings of frustration and unhappiness, then it is verily man's condition never to be satisfied.

In the following, consumer experiences characteristic of our truly nondurable goods will *not* be compared, I hasten to add, to those of various animals with similar goods. Rather, these experiences will be compared to those made by humans with other categories of goods and services. It is in this manner that the differential, commodity-specific incidence of consumer disappointment can best be evaluated. Such comparisons will

---

[8] Edward Young perhaps started this genre by writing in *Night Thoughts* (1742):

Is it, that things terrestrial can't content?
Deep in rich pasture, will thy flocks complain?
Not so; but to their master is deny'd
To share their sweet serene. (Night VII, lines 36–40)

Samuel Johnson is much more meticulous in *Rasselas* (1759):

What . . . makes the difference between man and all the rest of the animal creation? Every beast that strays beside me has the same corporal necessities with myself; he is hungry and crops the grass, he is thirsty and drinks the stream, his thirst and hunger are appeased, he is satisfied and sleeps; he rises again and is hungry, he is again fed and is at rest. I am hungry and thirsty like him, but when thirst and hunger cease I am not at rest; I am, like him, pained with want, but am not, like him, satisfied with fulness. (Chapter II)

Finally, in Leopardi's "Canto Notturno di un pastore errante dell' Asia" (1830) the act of eating is no longer specifically mentioned, but it is implied to have just taken place in the following lines where the shepherd speaks to his flock:

When in the shade you lie upon the grass,
You are tranquil and content,
And yet I sit upon the grass, and in the shade,
And weariness invades my mind. (Translation by John Humphreys
    Whitfield, *Canti,* Naples: Scalabrini, 1962, p. 175.)

be attempted with respect to consumer durables in the next section, and with respect to various types of services in the one following.

Consumer Durables

If Scitovsky is right in holding that comfort is the enemy of pleasure, then any good that assures comfort or keeps discomfort at bay in a durable fashion, such as an automatic heating system or a refrigerator, will yield a comparatively low amount of pleasure. As long as it is in working order, such a good will satisfy a need once and for all, so that pleasure is experienced only once, when the good is first acquired and put to use ("turned on"). Thereafter, comfort is assured, but the pleasure that comes with traveling from discomfort to comfort is no longer available. There is a good expression for this state of affairs: we say that the particular good has come to be taken for granted. Implicit in this expression is a slight reproach or regret—we feel that we should be more happy, grateful, and freshly pleased about having the good than we really are. To achieve an appropriately appreciative state of mind we can either work on our imagination—try to get back, each time we use the good (or each time we remember it is in use) into the same state of mind as when we first acquired it—or, less commendably, we can work up feelings of relative superiority and think of the poor fellows who haven't got it quite yet. But these sorts of mental exercises are still unlikely to generate the acute pleasure that is experienced when a needed or useful good is first acquired and put to use. In truth, the refrigerator already comes close to yielding as little active pleasure as much older, similarly most useful objects and inventions such as plate glass or, for that matter, the wheel.

Actually when we say that we take certain of these permanently comfort-yielding durable goods for granted, we may well address a reproach not only to ourselves, but to the goods in question. We fault them precisely for being all comfort and hardly any pleasure, in sharp contrast to more traditional purchases of nondurables such as food. Goods that yield considerable pleasure along with comfort have taken up the bulk of consumer purchases for many centuries; they also stand in the center of the consumption experience of childhood and youth. Hence, the drastic change in the *balance of pleasure and comfort* that comes with durables is unforeseen and the small amount of pleasure they yield is initially disconcerting.[9] As time passes consumers will presumably come to accept that in the case of durables the pleasure-comfort balance is different from that of nondurables: they will learn to trade off comfort against pleasure and otherwise adjust their expectations. To some extent, each generation may have to go through this process inasmuch as consumption experiences during adulthood are more heavily weighted with durables than those during childhood. But if our analysis is right, disappointment could be especially widespread in a society in which mass diffusion of durables first occurs. This is of course quite paradoxical, since one might expect a population to be in a fine mood when large parts of it accede for the first time to the much celebrated, Rostovian blessings of "high mass consumption." In actual fact both moods, general optimism and widespread disaffection, could be encountered in rapid succession. They also could exist side by side, as when the older generation successfully represses any disappointment with its life-style and emphasizes the material progress it has achieved, while the younger generation has no empathy for that experience and denounces the emptiness of the parents' lives. As a result of these contrasting moods, the period of transition to "high mass consumption" could be politically quite volatile.

Having made my major point with regard to durables I must qualify it. To divide all consumer goods into durables

[9] The argument is somewhat analogous to, though hopefully less speculative and more convincing than, the notion of some anthropologists that *homo sapiens* is still primarily programmed by evolution as the hunter and gatherer he was for several hundreds of millennia and that his maladjustments are to be attributed to his having taken up sedentary occupations just a few thousand years ago.

and nondurables exaggerates the difference in disappointment potential between these two categories. From the point of view of the pleasure-comfort balance it is useful to distinguish between three subcategories of durables: (1) those that are in continuous use—the house or apartment, heating or air conditioning systems, refrigerators, etc.; (2) those that are in use at regular cyclical or generally predictable intervals because their use is tied in with the natural rhythm and structure of everyday life—the car (when it is used for utilitarian transportation such as driving to work, shopping, etc.), washing machines, dishwashers, etc.; (3) those that are used at irregular intervals in accordance with whether the owners "feel like" using them—hi-fi equipment, piano, camera, the car to the extent it is used purely for the sake of getting "driving pleasure," and so on.[10]

What has been said about the disappointment-generating characteristic of durables—that they are more weighted with comfort than pleasure in comparison with traditional purchases—applies most strongly to the first category of durables, somewhat less so to the second, and least to the third. Durable articles that are used at the owner's whim are in many ways like nondurables: whenever the owner decides to use them, this is so because he or she derives pleasure or stimulation from them, as well as some comfort after use—as when the desire to take pictures or to play the piano has been pacified (or when boredom has been temporarily contained).

The durables of the third category can best be considered as consumer capital, similar to children's toys, that yield a stream of services rather similar, from the point of view of the potential for disappointment, to such nondurable purchases as a ticket to the opera or the stadium, a pleasure trip, or even an ice-cream cone. An important difference is, however, that once the services dispensed by the durable are no longer desired, the durable good itself still "hangs around"; thus it re-

---

[10] As with any classification, there are difficulties with neatly arranging all durables into the three categories. For example, does television belong to the second or third category? For the majority of viewers, who have developed the "TV habit," to the second.

minds the owner that it has ceased providing enjoyment and therefore continues to provoke a certain amount of disappointment. Children are in a better position than adults in this respect, as any excessively durable toy that no longer yields pleasure and stimulation will be "made to disappear" by the parents or destroyed by the children.

More will be said in the next chapter on the recurring hostility toward durable objects meant to provide pleasure and comfort. At this stage, however, I wish to argue that the first two categories of durables are especially prone to generating disappointment. These durables constitute the core of the modern household durable culture. That the pleasure-comfort balance is totally different from that normally experienced in conjunction with nondurables has already been noted for those durables (heating system, refrigerator, etc.) that are in continuous use. It is the characteristic homeostatic property of these articles that accounts for their ability to keep discomfort permanently at bay, with the counterpart that the pleasure-generating trip from discomfort to comfort is eliminated.

In the case of the second category of durables—those that are in use at regular intervals because their use is tied in with the rhythm and structure of everyday life—the homeostatic property is less pronounced as they still have to be set in motion and otherwise manipulated by their owners to yield their services. Washing machines and dishwashers, for example, still need to be at least "loaded," set in motion by their users, and unloaded, and some real if fleeting moment of pleasure is accordingly associated with such operations as well as with the pushing of the button. Also, the visible, effortless, and a bit wondrous transformation wrought by these machines—the turning of dirty objects into clean ones—produces some renewable pleasure. But what has been said about the peculiar comfort-pleasure balance of the first category of durables applies here too, if to a lower degree.

The most important modern durable good is the private automobile. It is of course still less homeostatic or automatic than the machines just noted. Also, there is no doubt that it can yield pleasure, "driving pleasure," either in connection

with its utilitarian function or even in pure form as when people take—or rather, used to take—a "joyride." The fact is that
the automobile provides, in Scitovsky's terms, "stimulation"
as well as want satisfaction: this is perhaps its unique strength
as a durable consumer good.[11] According to a well-known
French critic, the car is a "sublime object": "The mobility
without effort it provides makes for a kind of unreal happiness, with existence and responsibility in suspense."[12] All of
this can be granted, especially for the first time when "person
meets car." Nevertheless, the car's utilitarian function is eventually paramount; and its ability to carry out this function
tends to be taken for granted almost as rapidly as that of the
thermostat-equipped heating system to provide even heat.
The reason is that the need for transportation—pressing
though it may be—is very different from the body's need for
food, sleep, or sex. Each time I am hungry I get genuine, indefinitely renewable pleasure from filling my stomach (a process well illustrated by the German proverb "appetite is the
best cook"), but the excitement and pleasure I get from my
car's ability to satisfy my (nonphysiological) need for transportation wanes rather rapidly. Here lies perhaps an important reason for the remarkable success of higher-priced and
luxury cars. Such cars are precisely meant to enhance the
stimulation function in relation to the want satisfaction function of the automobile. As a recent advertisement for a BMW
blurts it out: "MEETING THE DEMANDS OF SOCIETY
[read: safety and antipollution devices, fuel economy] IS NO
EXCUSE FOR BUILDING A BORING CAR." Many con-
sumers thus strive to fight the disappointment that they sense
will be connected with the purely utilitarian aspect of the car
by spending more on the vehicle than is strictly necessary for
transportation purposes. In this manner, they obtain both a
somewhat superior driving experience and the satisfaction of
feeling superior to the great mob of motorists. They are will-

---

[11] Some kitchen appliances have a similar ability to rise above pure
utility and to provide stimulation, in particular the modern food proces-
sor.

[12] Jean Baudrillard, *Le système des objets* (Paris: Gallimard, 1968), p.
94.

ing to spend a substantial amount of money on tilting the pleasure-comfort balance of their purchase in the direction of more pleasure. For exactly the same reason, they have long tolerated—perhaps desired—a certain amount of "built-in obsolescence": a new automobile makes for a radical shift in the pleasure-comfort balance.

Another distinction may be made between durable goods that, when bought, are totally finished and are not supposed to be given any sort of individual touch by the consumer and those that permit or even require that touch. By far the most important item in the latter category is of course the individually owned house or apartment, while the conventional consumer durables, from car to washing machine, belong in the former. The difference between these two categories from the point of view of pleasure generation and maintenance is fairly obvious: when owners have the opportunity, as with a house, to furnish, arrange and rearrange it, to repair, improve, or even to add to it, they in effect make it into a reflection of themselves. The pleasure yielded by the house is immeasurably enhanced by the narcissistic contemplation of the result of their own efforts and choices. Here is an important way of counteracting the loss of pleasure that would otherwise follow upon the permanent-comfort-producing acquisition of a house.[13] However, this remedy against pleasure loss is typically not available to consumers in relation to their more modern purchases that "come" complete and just have to be "plugged in." The only change which they can experience is not a further transformation or improvement in accordance with the special needs or tastes of the individual consumer, but a breakdown which, once again, does not permit the

[13] This is also true of personal belongings that undergo substantial change simply as a result of use. A marvelous account is in Diderot's essay "Regrets on an Old Robe or Advice to Those Who Have More Taste than Wealth": "Why did I not keep it? It was made for me; I was made for it. . . . When the thick ink would not flow from my pen, it offered its side. Long black streaks testified to the frequent service it had given me. These long streaks proclaimed the *littérateur,* the writer, the man who works. At present [in my new robe], I look like a rich *fainéant;* one does not know who I am." Diderot, *Oeuvres* (Paris: Pléiade, 1935), p. 733.

owner to intervene—by "fixing it" himself he would regenerate the pleasure received from the article—but obliges him to call in a specialist repairman at great cost. With the automobile, the second most important possession of the average citizen, there is at least the possibility of keeping up its appearance, and it is perhaps this desire to make it "one's own" and to derive from it the concomitant narcissistic pleasure, that pushes so many car owners to spend a large portion of their free weekend time on washing it and on shining it up. The case of sports cars and motorcycles comes close to that of the owner-occupied house in that the owners of these vehicles tend to take full and enthusiastic charge of maintenance as well as of all kinds of modifications and additions. Finally, an extraordinary instance of the propensity to make assembly-line standard objects into wholly personal creations is the phenomenon of the "Lowriders" in San Francisco and elsewhere in the West. Here the Chicano and other Spanish-speaking communities have invented a parade, held primarily on weekend evenings, of older, originally quite nondescript cars that have been totally transformed into outlandish, garish, highly personal vehicles that boast a special type of low suspension (hence "Lowriders") and are "customized" in many other respects. Such cars are part of a "life-style" that is an open protest against the "square," pleasure-poor world of the usual utility vehicle.

A closer look at various categories of durable goods leaves intact the point made earlier when all durables were contrasted with nondurables: the modern, mass-produced durable consumer good subverts the way in which consumers extracted pleasure from their purchases in the predurable era. Along with their extraordinarily useful services, these goods are likely to generate a great deal of vaguely felt disappointment, particularly at the time of their first massive diffusion in a society.[14]

[14] An influential article by a British sociologist has pointed to another possible source of resentment against durables. In the case of workers, the acquisition of durables (including automobiles) precipitates and symbolizes a change in the "image of society" from a class-struggle *or* a tra-

Services

In the advanced capitalist countries of the West, an important shift in the occupational structure has taken place in recent decades. Employment in the so-called service sector, that congeries of activities comprising not only finance and commerce, but educational, health, recreational, professional, and government services, has grown much faster than employment in industry and agriculture. As a consequence, so it has been proclaimed, our economy has become a "Service Economy" (Victor Fuchs) and our society a "Post-Industrial Society" (Daniel Bell).

The expansion of the service sector has as its counterpart an increase in consumers' expenditures on services, particularly in such fields as education, health, and recreation. To the extent that governments provide such services, actual expenditures are replaced by higher general and social security taxes (or stronger inflationary pressures); the direct link between the rendering of a service and the monetary quid pro quo is thereby severed. Nevertheless, the existence of these services and the fact that one has paid taxes (or suffered inflation) to support them create expectations of entitlement. Regardless of the institutional arrangement, it is therefore possible to speak of a new and increasingly important category of consumer purchases.[15] It will now be argued, as earlier with consumer

---

ditional-reverential image to a privatized, pecuniary image of social relationships. Such a change brings with it a sense of loss, and some of the blame for that loss will attach to the newly acquired gadgets. See David Lockwood, "Sources of Variation in Working-Class Images of Society," *Sociological Review* 14 (Nov. 1966), 249–267, reprinted in Martin Bulmer, ed., *Working-Class Images of Society* (London: Routledge and Kegan Paul, 1975), pp. 16–31, particularly p. 23.

[15] The shares in the consumer budget of actual spending on services remained constant in Great Britain, as was shown by J. I. Gershuny, in his study "The Self-Service Economy," *New Universities Quarterly* (Summer 1977), 50–66. But a proper accounting should include welfare state services that were received by the consumer without immediate cash counterpart. There can be no doubt that, with this sort of accounting, the

durables, that the disappointment potential of these purchases is likely to be quite high.

The reasons, however, are very different. In the case of consumer durables, the trouble was not their performance, which on the whole is rather reliable, but their failure to yield "pleasure" to the extent consumers were expecting on the basis of their prior experience with nondurable purchases. In the case of health and educational services, on the other hand, performance itself is notably uneven and unpredictable; here one new and jarring experience, in comparison with more traditional purchases, is the high degree of variability in the quality and efficacy of the thing acquired. As a result, the large numbers who lose out in this particular lottery are likely to be an unhappy and disappointed lot.

Once again, the likelihood of disappointment is greatest for the first generation of consumers of these services, that is, for consumers who approach these purchases with the expectations about reliability and predictability of the product that have been formed during the many years in which they purchased mostly apples, eggs, shoes, refrigerators, and such. Thus, it is again the upwardly mobile groups brimming over with new consumption ambitions who will bear the brunt of the disappointment as they painfully learn about the much higher degree of risk and uncertainty associated with services which they are now anxious to try out. Nevertheless, even after considerable experience with the risk involved in these service purchases, the disappointment potential remains high for the many who simply refuse to comprehend that educators, physicians, and psychiatrists are entitled to large payments (in fees or via taxes) in exchange for services whose efficacy can be so far off the mark.

The argument about the high disappointment potential of these services becomes a great deal stronger in times when a substantial effort is made to expand rapidly the supply of these services with the intention of making them more widely

---

share of expenditures for services would show a substantial increase particularly for those items—health and education—that are of major interest for the present study.

available. Under these conditions, their *average quality* is likely to drop substantially. This is so in part because it is difficult to assemble at the same time all the inputs needed for high quality performance—new school buildings are built faster than new teachers are formed, or vice versa. It is therefore precisely when a society makes a determined effort to widen access to certain services that the quality of these services will decline, with obvious negative effects on the morale of both new and old consumers.[16]

The drop in quality consequent upon expansion is a peculiar characteristic of certain services and does not apply to consumer durables or to other services, at least not nearly to the same extent. The principal reason is that the tolerance for quality decline is much wider, for example, in the case of educational services than for industrial goods such as refrigerators or for high-technology services, such as airplane travel. An expansion in airplane travel or in the production of refrigerators cannot take place unless all or most essential inputs are available in appropriate quantities, whereas newly expanded higher education services can be and typically are offered *in spite* of unresolved bottlenecks, that is, with unprepared teachers, impossibly crowded classrooms, or other such imbalances.

The likelihood of a disappointing performance of newly established or expanded services is reinforced by some further observations. In the first place, when certain social services like education are expanded so as to cater to newly emerging social groups, it may not be appropriate to offer exactly the same services as have been previously supplied to the traditional "educated class." Hence even without quality decline, and precisely because there has been no change or adaptation, the services might be ineffective and meet with resistance. Again, a period of learning and mutual adjustment will be needed.

Secondly, there is a class of services for which a strong de-

[16] For a fuller treatment of this and the following points, see my article "The Welfare State in Trouble: Systemic Crisis or Growing Pains?" *American Economic Review* 70 (May 1980), 113–116.

mand may arise in advance of real knowledge about how to satisfy it; recent examples are day-care facilities and psychotherapeutic services. What happens in these situations is that, in response to an effective market demand, some members of society come forward proclaiming, like any good hustler, "We can handle this for you," but actually only begin to learn "on the job," in the process of rendering these newly popular services as best they can. A great deal has been written about consumer ignorance and the resulting asymmetrical situation of consumer and producer.[17] In the present case, producers are just as ignorant as consumers, at least during the earlier stages of their operation. It is the supplier's ignorance rather than his wiles that accounts for the poor quality of services rendered. Again, the resulting consumer disappointment is engendered by the peculiar marketability of certain services in spite of quality being much lower than expected.

Grounded as it is in a variety of converging situations and characteristics, the disappointment potential of certain newly expanded social services has by now assumed a rather formidable look. In fact, the argument here developed amounts to one way of understanding what is sometimes called "the Crisis of the Welfare State." The feeling is widespread today that the attempt at making capitalism compatible with the eradication of poverty and unemployment and with a more equal distribution of income and of life chances has been increasingly running into inflationary and other troubles in a number of countries. The explanation of this development has generally been sought in some deep-seated "structural" characteristics of Western societies. In this vein, James O'Connor has written about the contradiction between the accumulation and the legitimation function of the capitalist state,[18] while

---

[17] See Kenneth J. Arrow, "Social Responsibility and Economic Efficiency," *Public Policy* 21 (Summer 1973), 303–318, and George Akerlof, "The Market for 'Lemons': Quality Uncertainty and the Market Mechanism," *Quarterly Journal of Economics* 85 (August 1970), 488–500.

[18] See James O'Connor, *The Fiscal Crisis of the State* (New York: St. Martin's Press, 1975).

Fred Hirsch has pointed to the impossibility of ever-increasing numbers of people acceding to what are strictly finite opportunities and types of enjoyment.[19] In contrast, the perspective here proposed does not look at the difficulties of the Welfare State as the reflection of "fundamental contradictions" or of absolute ceilings; rather, it sees these difficulties as serious, but quite possibly temporary growing pains. These pains may well cause considerable trouble when first encountered, but can eventually be brought under control as a result of various learning experiences and mutual adjustments. Hence our message on these matters is rather less dismal than other diagnoses that have achieved a great deal of notoriety.

What happens to the disappointment that is generated by the various unhappy experiences that have been reviewed? One possibility is that customers (or patients) will become angry at the institutions, firms, or individuals that supply disappointing goods or services, and will clamor for improvement and reform. Recent history indeed provides several illustrations of this outcome, for example with respect to educational services in Western Europe.

But anger at the supplier is not the only conceivable reaction. In the case of psychotherapy, for example, the patient must complement the psychotherapist's services by some input of his own. Thus the reason for the meager result of his visits to the therapist could well lie in the inadequacy of his own contributions. In this case, the disappointment the purchaser feels could well be turned against himself. This mutation of disappointment with the thing purchased and with the seller into *disappointment with oneself* could also occur in connection with other services that involve some collaboration on the part of the recipient—for example, in the case of educational and various professional services, as indeed with any purchase that requires discrimination on the part of the buyer.[20]

[19] See Fred Hirsch, *Social Limits to Growth* (Cambridge, Mass.: Harvard University Press, 1976).

[20] Some advertisements are meant to convince prospective buyers that they will become beautiful or lovable as a result of purchasing some

It is interesting to speculate whether paying for services directly or indirectly (through taxes) would influence the degree of disappointment that is likely to arise. On the one hand, direct payment should make the customers more critical and quality-conscious than if the service is supplied without an immediate cash quid pro quo. On the other hand, the very fact of payment often sets up the presumption that one *must* have received an adequate countervalue, so that people will tend to blame themselves (and remain silent) if the outcome of the transaction is unsatisfactory. It is perhaps in part because of this strange psychological mechanism that publicly financed services are so much more frequently and strongly criticized than those rendered on a private basis.

It may be useful to review the argument that has been developed in this chapter. Consumption experiences, so it has been shown, yield dissatisfaction and disappointment along with satisfaction. It was first argued that the *truly* nondurable goods (such as food), which necessarily forfeit their physical shape through consumption, hold a privileged position as being peculiarly pleasure-intensive and disappointment-resistant. Then, the argument has focused on two specific categories of consumer purchases, durables and services, which have greatly gained in importance in recent decades, and whose disappointment potential is shown to be high. Quite different reasons apply in each case. With respect to durables, disappointment originates primarily in the fact that the balance between pleasure and comfort provided by these goods is tilted much more toward comfort (and against pleasure) than is the case for nondurables. With respect to services, disappointment arises out of the large number of cases—in comparison with goods purchases—in which there is a partial or total failure to achieve the purpose for which the services are acquired, particularly in the case of educational, medical, and other professional services. Moreover, if such services are suddenly

---

product, but at the same time manage to intimate that, if the desired transformation does not take place, those buyers have only themselves to blame. See Arthur A. Leff, *Swindling and Selling* (New York: Free Press, 1975), pp. 157–175.

offered—in response to social pressures—in much larger quantities than before, their average quality is likely to suffer and the intended beneficiaries of the expansion will be disgruntled rather than grateful.

It is a characteristic of all these findings that they apply with special force to periods when important progressive changes are taking place, with new groups gaining access to goods and services previously reserved for the few or not available at all. Disappointment arises typically because new types of purchases are undertaken with the kinds of expectations that consumers have come to associate with more traditional purchases.

CHAPTER 3

The General Hostility
Toward New Wealth

One leading aim of this study, as developed in the preceding chapter, is to learn about the strength and shape of consumer disappointment by looking at *specific* categories and *differential* characteristics of various goods and services. While I believe that this approach has considerable further potential, I shall now go in the more aggregative direction. The reason is that, in the course of searching for disappointment, I have found more than I was looking for; and I have come across much evidence that, in the West, each time economic progress has enlarged the availability of consumer goods for some strata of society, strong feelings of disappointment in, or of hostility toward, the new material wealth have come to the fore. Along with appreciation, infatuation, and even addiction, affluence seems to produce its own backlash, almost regardless of what *kinds* of goods are newly and more abundantly marketed.

Clearly, a major historical investigation would be required fully to document this broad conjecture. Here I shall only exhibit a few pieces of evidence, primarily from the eighteenth century, to be followed by a discussion of some of the principal arguments that seem to feed, time and again, the hostility toward new wealth.

Historical Evidence from the
Eighteenth Century in England and France

My principal witness for the ambivalence with which the appearance and availability of greater material wealth have been greeted is the venerable Adam Smith.

His major work, entitled, as we all know, *An Inquiry into the Nature and Causes of the Wealth of Nations,* is of course centrally concerned with the achievement of greater wealth and with the economic policies needed to advance that objective. In the Introduction to the book he contrasts the "savage nations" that are "miserably poor" with the "civilized and thriving nations" where even the poorest "may enjoy a greater share of the *necessaries and conveniencies of life* than it is possible for any savage to acquire." So the book is conceived as an explanation of, and as a paean to, growth, wealth, and "opulence," and as an attack on policies obstructing the goal of providing everyone with "necessaries and conveniencies" aplenty.

How odd and surprising is it then to find, further on in *Wealth,* these same "conveniencies" referred to in the most disparaging terms! This is what happens, without having been duly noticed, in the well-known Chapter 4 of Book III, entitled "How the Commerce of Towns Contributed to the Improvement of the Country," where Smith describes how the appetite of the "great proprietors" for various domestic and imported manufactures led to the loosening of feudal ties. The feudal lords gave up their retainers and entered into longer-term contracts with their tenants in order to be able to acquire the goods offered by "merchants and artificers." This is described variously as an act of "folly" or as a selling of "their birthright," while the goods acquired in the process are characterized as "trinkets and baubles, fitter to be the play-things of children than the serious pursuits of men," or, for illustrative purposes, as "a pair of diamond buckles . . . or something as frivolous and useless."[1]

How to explain this sudden invective against the "conveniencies" whose diffusion is so intensely celebrated elsewhere in *Wealth?* Is it just an exception, a lapse, to be explained perhaps by Adam Smith's dislike of the feudal system and of its foremost representatives, the great lords? Such an interpretation will not do, for in *The Theory of Moral Sentiments* Smith uses very much the same derogatory language with respect to

[1] *Wealth of Nations* (Modern Library Edition), pp. 388–392.

the things money can buy, even though their purchasers are not now identified as lords foolishly giving up something precious in exchange, but as the general public. It is an important passage—Smith introduces here his famous metaphor of the "invisible hand" long before *Wealth*. He speaks of the desire for "trinkets of frivolous utility" on the part of "many people," including the "poor man's son whom heaven in its anger has visited with ambition." All of these persons operate under the influence of a *"deception* which arouses and keeps in continued motion the industry of mankind." This is the original invisible hand: the people whose decentralized activities it orchestrates are *not* pursuing their true self-interest; they are deceived in that regard, and the deception is truly huge as can be gauged from the kinds of ridiculous goods that are sought out by its victims. The "trinkets" and "baubles" are again very much in evidence, as well as adjectives such as "contemptible," "trifling," and "frivolous," and the specific objects that are named for illustrative purposes range from a watch to a "toothpick," an "ear picker," and a "machine for cutting the nails."[2] The final verdict is extremely harsh and has a somber, Hobbesian ring:

> Power and riches appear then to be ... enormous and operose machines contrived to produce a few trifling conveniencies to the body, ... [T]hough they may save [the owner] from some smaller inconveniencies, [they] can protect him from none of the severer inclemencies of the season. They keep off the summer shower, not the winter storm, but leave him always as much, and sometimes more, exposed than before to anxiety, to fear, and to sorrow; to diseases, to danger, and to death.[3]

All of man's striving for material betterment is thus dismissed as an elaborate charade in which the utmost energy is

[2] Adam Smith, *The Theory of Moral Sentiments,* edited by D. D. Raphael and A. L. Macfie (Oxford: Clarendon, 1976), pp. 180–185.

[3] *Moral Sentiments,* p. 302. See also Samuel Hollander, *The Economics of Adam Smith* (Toronto: University of Toronto Press, 1972), pp. 246–248.

expended by countless numbers of people in the pursuit of illusory goals.

The *Theory of Moral Sentiments* dates from 1759, and *Wealth of Nations* was published, after a long gestation, seventeen years later. The period during which Adam Smith maintained this strange animosity toward the material culture of his time, while celebrating economic progress and "public opulence" elsewhere in his work, was marked by slowly but significantly increasing commercial and industrial prosperity.[4] Such was certainly Adam Smith's own perception when he wrote of England that "the annual produce of its land and labour is, undoubtedly, much greater at present than it was either at the restoration or at the revolution." At this point, Smith is in his pro-opulence mood and, for once, finds some quite positive things to say about the accumulation of "things more durable." While again mentioning, besides buildings, furniture, books, etc., "things more frivolous, jewels, baubles, ingenious trinkets of various kinds," he here declares such disposition of one's income to be more useful than spending on "a profuse and sumptuous table" and on "maintaining a great number of menial servants." The reasons given are that durables will eventually trickle down to the less affluent, that spending on durables is more easily checked, if found excessive, and that such spending leads, directly and indirectly, to more employment.[5]

Thus Smith was literally of two minds with regard to the material culture of his time and to its increase. And his two views in this area are even harder to reconcile than his much better known ambivalence on the division of labor.[6] In my opinion, there is no need even to attempt a reconciliation: Smith's ambivalence reflects that of generation after generation of Western intellectuals both celebrating and vilifying

---

[4] Phyllis Deane and W. A. Coale, *British Economic Growth, 1688–1959,* 2nd ed. (Cambridge: Cambridge University Press, 1969), Chap. II.

[5] *Wealth,* pp. 328–332.

[6] E. G. West, "Adam Smith's Two Views on the Division of Labor," *Economica* 31 (February 1964), 23–32; Nathan Rosenberg, "Adam Smith and the Division of Labor: Two Views or One?" *Economica* 32 (February 1965), 127–139.

material progress! Those with a less protean mind than his simply have felt a stronger compulsion to be consistent, so that ordinarily we find one and the same person aligned with only one of the two opposite views.

What further evidence is there, from the mid-eighteenth century, for my point that antagonism toward material culture comes to the fore in periods of economic expansion when consumer goods, frequently of a new kind, become more widely diffused? For England, it is almost anticlimactic to add anything to the striking case of Adam Smith. There is no lack of outright and consistent condemnation of the new prosperity, often denoted by the still predominantly derogatory term "luxury," on the part of important figures, such as Bolingbroke, Swift, and Pope. Particularly strong attacks on luxury were successfully published in the increasingly prosperous third quarter of the eighteenth century: they include John Brown's *An Estimate of the Manners and Principles of the Times* (1757), a highly popular work, and Smollett's best known novel *The Expedition of Humphry Clinker* (1771).[7]

In France, at around the same time, the dominant spokesman against what we call today "consumerism" was of course Rousseau. Indeed, we find him inveighing against it from his famous first political tract, the *Discourse on the Sciences and the Arts,* all the way to the *Considerations on the Government of Poland,* which was his last major political work. He had a favorite word for denigrating the world of objects and durable commodities: *colifichet.* This is a derogatory term which designates a frivolous object that has little utility, is in rather poor taste, and is desired—often by frivolous women—out of vanity and social rivalry. *Colifichet* is used in the *Discourse* as well as in the *Considerations.*[8] In the latter, Rousseau makes a dis-

[7] These works by Brown and Smollett stand, respectively, in the center of two recent, detailed surveys of the luxury literature of eighteenth-century England: Simeon M. Wade, Jr., "The Idea of Luxury in Eighteenth-Century England," unpublished Ph.D. thesis, Department of History, Harvard University, 1968, and John Sekora, *Luxury: The Concept in Western Thought, from Eden to Smollett* (Baltimore: Johns Hopkins University Press, 1977).

[8] The term is also found in *L'Emile* and *La Nouvelle Héloïse,* always with the same derogatory meaning. Rousseau was so fond of using this

tinction between the *luxe des colifichets* and another kind of luxury, that of having many retainers who would receive their subsistence as well as their education from the lords. Just as Adam Smith thought the lords foolish to have exchanged their retainers for the trinkets and baubles of the towns, so did Rousseau exhort the Poles to opt—if they insist on having luxury—for the luxury of retainers in preference to that of *colifichets*.

Faithful reader and self-proclaimed pupil that he was of Rousseau, Robespierre later invented his own derogatory term for the world of material goods: *chétives marchandises,* meaning frail or shabby merchandise, a striking expression that has become famous and must have had shock and surprise value at a time when shortages of basic foods were widespread. Could it be, incidentally, that Robespierre, with *colifichet* preying on his memory, came up with *chétif,* a simple rearrangement of the last two syllables of Rousseau's favorite term? However that may be, he used the term in a speech in which he strongly disapproved of the looting of sugar and coffee from some Paris stores, in February 1793. His principal argument was that the revolutionary energies of the people must be reserved for more worthy purposes than the going after something as *chétif* as groceries.[9]

But back to the middle of the century. Before Rousseau, Quesnay and the Physiocrats had made their own distinction between varieties of luxury. It was not too different from that of Rousseau or, for that matter, from the one Adam Smith made subsequently between "trinkets" and a "profuse and sumptuous table." Quesnay distinguished between the luxury of durable objects, which he called *luxe de décoration,* and the lavish spending on food, which he called, a bit incongruously to our ears, *faste de subsistance.*[10] *Faste* conveys splendor and

---

rather quaint and unusual word that his works supply 3 of 9 illustrative quotations in Littré's Dictionary. For the use of *colifichet* in the *Discourse* and in *Considerations,* see *Oeuvres complètes* (Paris: NRF, Pléiade, 1964), Vol. III, pp. 51 and 965.

[9] *Oeuvres de Maximilien Robespierre* (Paris: Presses Universitaires de France, 1958), Vol. 9, p. 275.

[10] François Quesnay, *Physiocratie, ou Constitution naturelle du gouvernement le plus avantageux au genre humain* (Leyden-Paris, 1768), p. 68.

sumptuousness, particularly in conjunction with public cere-
monies, and escapes the association with sinfulness and corruption that had attached to *luxe* since the Middle Ages if not
earlier. Hence, by calling large expenses on food *faste* and
those on objects *luxe,* Quesnay underlined his opinion, similar
to that of Rousseau (but opposite to that of Adam Smith in his
pro-opulence mood), that spending lavishly on food was preferable to the amassing of objects. Some of the minor physiocrats, such as Nicolas Baudeau, elaborated at length on this
distinction and on the preference for the "truly nondurable"
goods I praised in Chapter 2.[11]

The physiocrats' reason for this preference for food over
objects was quite different from Rousseau's: it was dictated by
their doctrine, which held agriculture to be the only real
source of national wealth and relegated not only traders, but
also artisans—those responsible for the "luxe de décoration"—to the "sterile classes." But it is precisely significant
that several distinct arguments converged in fostering hostility
toward the world of objects at a time when this world was in
expansion.

A final, extreme, and metaphysical example of this hostility
comes from the correspondence of Madame du Deffand, the
remarkable eighteenth-century hostess of various brilliant
salons, who was eternally haunted by *ennui*. In a letter to
Horace Walpole, she speaks of her "very great desire to leave
this world" and gives as principal reason "the emptiness one
finds in all the objects by which one is surrounded."[12]

The distinction is made in the first observation following the *Tableau
économique* and holds therefore an important place in Quesnay's
thought. In the above-named edition of the work, the actually printed
terms are *luxe de subsistance* and *luxe de décoration,* but an erratum sheet
inserted at the beginning of the volume asks the reader to substitute *faste*
for *luxe* in *luxe de subsistance,* but not in *luxe de décoration.*

[11] Nicolas Baudeau, *Principes de la science morale et politique sur le
luxe et les loix somptuaires* (1767), reprinted in *Collection des économistes*
(Paris, Geuthner, 1912), pp. 26–32. See also Ellen Ross, "The Debate on
Luxury in Eighteenth-Century France," unpublished dissertation, Department of History, University of Chicago, 1975.

[12] Madame la Marquise du Deffand, *Lettres à Walpole, Voltaire et
quelques autres* (Paris: Plasma, 1979), p. 96. Letter written in 1773. See

Here, then, are some eighteenth-century bits of evidence from England and France for my conjecture. In the next century, as the industrial revolution resulted in an unprecedented flow of new goods and objects, various expressions of unhappiness with this flow are rather easy to collect. To Adam Smith's trinkets and baubles, Rousseau's *colifichets,* and Robespierre's *chétives marchandises,* Baudelaire was soon to add his horror of those people who are "fanatically devoted to the utensil" *(fanatiques de l'ustensile),* while Flaubert protested, at a time of rapid economic expansion under Napoleon III, against the new, cheap, mass-produced articles, in a typical outburst:

> We must shout against cheap gloves, against desk armchairs, against the mackintosh, against cheap stoves, against fake cloth, against fake luxury . . . ! Industry has developed ugliness in gigantic proportions![13]

But I do not really wish to pursue the matter into the nineteenth century. The job would be too massive and also, perhaps, unnecessary. For my major point is clear already: the recoil from "consumerism" is by no means an invention or a monopoly of the nineteen-sixties.

The Manifold Case against New Goods

This finding broadens our inquiry. It is of course conceivable that each time a new wave of consumer goods reaches the market, some specific characteristics of these goods arouse hostility (while others provoke the passionate desire to acquire them). That this can indeed be the case has been shown in

---

also Reinhard Kuhn, *The Demon at Noon-tide:* Ennui *in Western Literature* (Princeton: Princeton University Press, 1976), pp. 140–147.

[13] Baudelaire, *Oeuvres* (Paris: Pléiade, 1932), Vol. II, p. 130, and Flaubert, *Correspondance* (Paris: Conard, 1927), Vol. IV, p. 20. "Mackintosh" is in English in the French text. Letter of January 29, 1854. See also Chapter 9, entitled "The Fanaticism of Utensils: Bourgeois Culture as Mass Culture," in César Graña, *Bohemian versus Bourgeois* (New York: Basic Books, 1964).

connection with modern, mass-produced consumer durables as well as with certain services dispensed by the modern welfare state. But as long as the hostility phenomenon appears to repeat itself no matter what the nature of new goods, a quite simple hypothesis must also be entertained and examined: the hostility could be due to the newness of the goods as such as well as to their large-scale diffusion, for the first time, among certain new social groups.

This hypothesis now puts me squarely at odds with Tibor Scitovsky who, in his *Joyless Economy,* has sung the praises of novelty. There is no doubt that novel goods can provide "stimulus," temporary relief from boredom, pride in being a pioneering consumer, and other such pleasures. The trouble is that there are countervailing displeasures, discontents, and disappointments that are also intimately connected with novel goods and their diffusion.

That novelty is two-edged is not much of a discovery. After all, there are several words in the language that reflect the experience that the new is untrustworthy and can be disappointing: newfangled, untried, faddish, gadgety, gimmicky, apart from the various derogatory nouns, such as baubles, trinkets, *colifichets,* and so on, with which we have become acquainted. Moreover, even would-be neutral, generic terms for these goods, such as "object" or "thing," have a slightly derogatory tone to them. One thinks of de Gaulle contemptuously referring to the United Nations as *ce machin* (this gimmick). What, then, have been the main sources of hostility to new products?

The arguments invoked are numerous. Upon looking more closely, however, one finds that they are less scattered than might appear at first. For one thing, an early argument will often reappear later in a different guise. Also, some of the arguments can be grouped together because they contradict each other. This, by the way, does not necessarily weaken the case that is being made. To the contrary, the arguments will appeal to groups with opposite ideologies or interests. Two pairs of archetypal arguments will serve to illustrate these points.

The first pair hails from the long debate on luxury. The introduction and diffusion of new wealth, particularly in the form of new goods, have long been received with hostility on two very different grounds. One is that the new goods constitute a threat to the social order and hierarchy as inferior ranks of society get hold of them or covet them. This essentially conservative argument against luxury is perhaps the most ancient. There was a widespread conviction, fostered originally by the Roman historians themselves, that the diffusion of luxury had caused the decline of Rome. In all the major European countries sumptuary laws were issued from the late Middle Ages on, with the principal purpose of regulating dress and spending in such a way that every "order" would stay in its proper place. Since there are no regulations with regard to new goods, they can become diffused to all ranks much more easily than those that are under regulation: a *nouveau riche*, that agent of social disintegration, is typically someone who is decked out in all kinds of novelties.

That new goods should be a menace to social stability because the "lower orders" can get hold of them and, as a result, might forget to stay in their proper place, strikes us today as a bit farfetched; but the proposition was reaffirmed not so long ago (in 1962) by the always insightful Frank Tannenbaum, who asserted that the "mechanical gadgets" pioneered in the United States, from automobiles to "toothpaste, fountain pens, and modern plumbing," would have a truly subversive, revolutionary impact on the "class-ridden and stratified societies . . . characteristic of Latin America and of much of the rest of the world."[14]

A similar observation was actually made as early as 1922 by the French political geographer André Siegfried, who saw the United States as "presiding at a general reorganization of the ways of living throughout the entire world" and therefore as "the terrible instigator of social change and revolution."[15] At this point one cannot help thinking of Marx and Schumpeter, who had of course stressed the profoundly revolutionary character of the capitalist system. But their emphasis was on the

---

[14] *Ten Keys to Latin America* (New York: Knopf, 1962), p. 203.
[15] Quoted in David M. Potter, *People of Plenty* (Chicago: University of Chicago Press, 1954), p. 135.

continuous upheavals the system generates in the techniques and organization of *production,* not on the contribution of ever widening *consumption* horizons to the undermining of the established order.

Very different and much more familiar is the next argument, making for hostility toward the New: one notes that the new articles are being primarily obtained, at first in any event, by the upper and wealthier classes; hence, these articles stand accused of increasing the visible gap between rich and poor. Moreover, to the extent that a static, zero-sum view of social wealth is widely entertained (whether or not such a view is justified), the new acquisitions of the rich are perceived to be made at the expense of the poor who would then be worse off not only in relative, but also in absolute terms. Rousseau put the point graphically when he wrote: "we need stock in our kitchens; that's why so many sick people lack broth. We need cordials on our table; that's why the peasant drinks only water. We need powder on our wigs; that's why so many poor have no bread." His conclusion: "If there were no luxury, there would not be any poverty."[16] Again, this idea has recurred time and again, in various forms. To cite a contemporary example: industrialization of the developing countries has been criticized because of its alleged unequalizing effect on income distribution. According to a frequent allegation, the output of the newly established industries of these countries goes primarily to the upper and middle classes. This argument has been a mainstay in the anti-industrialization backlash that has been a strong intellectual current, particularly in Latin America, since the mid-sixties. And it has even been argued that absolute impoverishment of the poor is a consequence, or else a precondition, of a certain type of industrialization.[17]

---

[16] *Oeuvres complètes,* Vol. III, p. 79 (in the *Last Reply* to various critical observations on his *Discourse on Arts and Sciences*).

[17] For a fuller treatment, see Hirschman, *A Bias for Hope: Essays on Development and Latin America* (New Haven: Yale University Press, 1971), Chap. 3, and *Essays in Trespassing: Economics to Politics and Beyond* (Cambridge: Cambridge University Press, 1981), Chap. 5.

New material wealth is, then, placed in a double bind: if it filters down to the masses, the conservatives are aroused because it threatens the social order. If it does not filter down, the progressives are appalled by the widening disparity in consumption standards. And, since the evidence is never unambiguous, new products and wealth can be and often have been accused and accursed on both counts.

Another kind of double bind, perhaps an even stronger one, results from two further elements in the discontent provoked by new products. We are already familiar with one of these elements: according to Adam Smith's formulation, the new contrivances "keep off the summer shower, but not the winter storm."[18] They are unable to change in any way the tragic and frightening characteristics of the human predicament, such as anxiety, sorrow, disease, or death. From this existential vantage point, the frantic effort made by people to acquire "trifling" objects always seems disproportionate to the result achieved. And even when objects are acquired to keep at bay another basic human affliction, namely, boredom or *ennui,* the situation is similar: the time during which any one object can truly amuse us is strictly limited; and because objects acquired for the purpose of countering boredom reveal in rather short order their inability to do so in any durable fashion, yet continue to "hang around," they themselves come to exude the boredom they have been unable to conquer. The rage over ennui is directed at them, as in Madame de Deffand's letter.

It is possible that eighteenth-century novelty was particularly exposed to this sort of existential criticism. Both the usefulness and the boredom-dispelling capability of novel objects increased considerably in the next two centuries, with such remarkable innovations as railroad, automobile, and airplane travel, the movies, radio, and television, not to speak of medical advances. Nevertheless, the basic strictures of Adam Smith and Madame du Deffand continue to apply: as I have attempted to show in the preceding chapter, there is still disap-

---

[18] As cited above, p. 48.

pointment in store for consumers as they acquire the more characteristic novelties of our day.

The Smith-Deffand critique aims at *deflating* the claims made on behalf of new products that appear on the consumers' horizon and excite their expectations and hopes. But there is another critique which goes in the opposite direction: the things proposed to us are not downgraded and shown up as futile and trifling; rather, their importance is *inflated* as they are denounced as potentially disastrous, and their invention or manufacture as impious. This sort of critique is probably the oldest of the lot. It is implied in a series of fundamental myths, from the Fall and Expulsion from Paradise to Prometheus's punishment for the invention of fire, and from Pandora's Box to the hydra-headed monster. These myths all center on the concept of Forbidden Knowledge and on the disasters that are in store for us if we try to pierce it.[19] In a remarkable reversal, the things which man invents and produces are suddenly turning from frivolous and trifling to extraordinarily threatening and sacrilegious.

It might be thought that, because of secularization and scientific progress, at least this particular critique of the world of objects is a thing of the past. Nothing could be farther from the truth. A modern version of the ancient concept of forbidden knowledge is very much with us, in the guise of the negative and noxious side effects of various, initially much-hailed, mass-produced novelty products—effects such as air pollution due to automobile traffic, health impairment following the use of "wonder drugs," and even the loss of economic and political independence because of reliance on imported raw materials. The idea is about, in consequence, that every advance creates more problems, as a result of these side effects, than it solves. Here is a modern, "scientific" way of reverting to the ancient thought, embodied in some of our most important myths, that dire consequences will follow if man's quest for knowledge proceeds unchecked.

[19] C. Ginzburg, "High and Low: The Theme of Forbidden Knowledge in the Sixteenth and Seventeenth Centuries," *Past & Present* 73 (November 1976), 28–41.

It is even conceivable that some new products could have the dubious distinction of being simultaneously the targets of the two apparently contradictory critiques that I have briefly recalled: they could be "trifling" as innovations and conveniences, yet have most serious environmental or ecological side effects. It is in fact not at all difficult to think of just such objects (for example, nonbiodegradable plastic containers, or household sprays that threaten the ozone layer of the atmosphere).

Nothing proves, of course, that the problems induced by technical advance necessarily form a divergent series, so that doom is not firmly assured as yet. It does seem to be the case, however, that the new products that are being poured out by industrial society and are finding acceptance because of their usefulness-at-first-sight will reveal whatever disadvantages or negative side effects they may harbor only slowly, as a result of repeated and prolonged use by masses of people. Subsequent product improvements to deal with the side effects may well be possible, but this whole process implies that the first generations of users serve as guinea pigs for the subsequent ones without being asked whether they are willing to play that role. A net social benefit probably results from each generation being tricked, as it were, into benefiting the next in this involuntary way. If all the noxious side effects were in full view from the beginning, consumers and public authorities might not permit technical progress to unfold.[20] The social cost of the process, however, is not only the actual damage inflicted by the side effects on the guinea pig generation, but the disgruntlement of the consumers once they find out about the not-so-wonderful characteristics of their new purchases.

Such, then, are some of the manifold discontents, hostilities, and disappointments aroused by the diffusion of new material wealth. My list is not and is not meant to be exhaustive. But I must still refer to a recent argument that has achieved consid-

[20] This is an illustration of what I have called the Principle of the Hiding Hand in *Development Projects Observed* (Washington: Brookings Institution, 1967), Chap. 1.

erable circulation and is now sometimes presented as the only conceivable reason for consumer disappointment.

In *Social Limits to Growth* Fred Hirsch has pointed to a special kind of disparity between expectations and reality that affects progressive societies. In such societies, the upwardly mobile consumer will expect that, when he is able to afford certain desired goods, these goods will yield the same satisfaction as they were perceived to yield when he could not afford them as yet. The trouble is, according to Hirsch, that many of these goods are either available only in limited quantities (as in the case of Impressionist paintings) or that their enjoyment depends critically on not being sought out by too many people at the same time (as in the case of some *quiet* beach resort).[21] Hence, as a large new group of hopeful, newly affluent consumers is ready to vie for such goods, they will find either (in the case of the Impressionist paintings) that prices have shot up disproportionately so that these goods are more than ever out of their reach, or that they are now purchasing a vacation on an impossibly crowded and polluted rather than on a quiet beach. Hirsch has used the term "positional goods" for these goods because, to some extent at least, they are acquired to signal something about the purchaser's position on the social scale. While such goods have been amply discussed long ago by Veblen under the rubric "conspicuous consumption"—and indeed by Adam Smith in an important passage of the *Theory of Moral Sentiments*[22]—Hirsch has made a real contribution by pointing out that these goods are often like will-o'-the-wisps in that they beckon the consumer on to exertion and effort only to elude him when he thinks he has made enough material progress to have them in his grasp.

Frustrating though this experience may be, it does not seem to me to constitute the major disappointment to which the consumer of economically progressive societies is exposed. By emphasizing situations in which the consumer is disgruntled

---

[21] For some earlier remarks in this vein, see Bertrand de Jouvenel, *Arcadia, Essais sur le mieux vivre* (Paris: S.E.D.E.I.S., 1968), p. 178 and *passim*.

[22] Page 50.

because he *fails* to get what he thought would be within his reach, Hirsch has overlooked, so it seems to me, the profound truth of Shaw's famous remark, "There are two tragedies in life. One is not to get your heart's desire. The other is to get it." What Shaw had in mind here was of course man's basic incapacity (or unwillingness) ever to achieve contentment. But there is no need for this "human nature" interpretation. Quite specific disappointments and discontents—the ones that have been reviewed in this and the preceding chapter—lie in store for consumers who, having achieved economic advance, are perfectly able to acquire the very goods they have set their hearts on. "Not to get your heart's desire," because the price of the goods which you were planning to acquire has shot out of sight, may actually be a good thing if the task at hand is to promote old-fashioned growth; for the failure to have achieved their consumption goals could spur upwardly mobile consumers to new and more aggressive efforts. The more serious disappointments which make consumers doubt the value of their exertions are those that come from experience with goods that are available and affordable, but simply do not yield the sort of satisfactions which were expected from them.

There is no intention here to deny the reality of the phenomenon Hirsch has pointed out. But once the many different kinds of disappointment incident to consumption have been brought into view, the Hirsch variety turns out to be just the tip of an iceberg. Its bulk has remained invisible for so long because the concept of disappointment did not fit the established categories of our economic discourse.

CHAPTER 4

From Private Concerns into
the Public Arena—I

The next step in my inquiry is easy enough to formulate as a question, namely: what happens as a result of all that disappointment in, and hostility toward, private consumption that is being generated? As already announced, I shall explore whether it makes sense to answer: a turn by the disappointed and hostile consumer-citizen to public action, a new concentration of energies on public concerns.

To make this answer *vaguely* plausible it may be helpful to appeal to another segment of the story. When for one reason or another participation in the *public* arena proves disappointing, a retreat into purely private concerns seems an obvious response that hardly requires justification. Certainly one would not expect perfect symmetry in these matters. But if the move from public to private seems so self-evident after the public sphere has given rise to disappointment, there is some reason to think that, in the opposite situation, the pendulum will swing the other way, though quite possibly with less force and certainty.

Exit and Voice Reactions to
Consumer Disappointment

But this sort of appeal to analogy and symmetry is not good enough. Actually, a more direct understanding of the turn from private to public concerns can be derived from quite elementary propositions of conventional economic theory. When a consumer has purchased apples and oranges during period 1 and oranges have been more disappointing to him than apples, then in period 2, other things being equal, he will

buy more apples. This sort of reasoning applies also to very
large aggregates of consumer spending, such as durables vs.
nondurables, or goods vs. services. The first reaction to disappointment with the sorts of modern services whose effectiveness suffers from considerable unreliability is to return to a
more traditional pattern of expenditures. There is much in-
trospective and anecdotal evidence that such shifts in expen-
diture patterns take place in the lives of individuals and
families, and it would be interesting to know whether oscillations of the postulated type can be detected for society as
a whole, or whether the individual oscillations tend to cancel
out.

But I am interested in an even grander shift. If important
private consumption experiences that had been particularly
looked forward to as presumed dispensers of "happiness"
leave behind them a trail of disappointment and frustration
and if, at the same time, a wholly different "pursuit of happiness," say, political action, is available to the disappointed
consumer, is it likely that this pursuit will be taken up at some
favorable occasion?

I believe this is a plausible contention. It is a straightforward deduction from conventional theory *provided* we deal
with consumers who are also conscious of being citizens and
who live in a culture where the private and the public are important dichotomous categories permanently vying for the attention and time of the "consumer-citizen." In a trenchant critique of Hannah Arendt's advocacy of the public life as man's
highest calling, Benjamin Schwartz argued some years ago
that a number of important societies such as the Chinese had
long done quite well without any conception at all of the public as distinct from the private good.[1] In such a culture it
would simply not occur to the disappointed consumer to turn
to public action; a principal alternative that would be open to
him instead would be to find satisfaction in the course exactly
opposite to the one he has been pursuing—that is, in the *de-
cumulation* of worldly belongings, in the attempt progres-

---

[1] "The Religion of Politics: Reflections on the Thought of Hannah
Arendt," *Dissent* 17 (March-April 1970), 146.

sively to reduce the intensity of his ambitions, desires, and even sensations. Such is indeed the Buddhist ideal.[2]

But wherever the public sphere is sensed as *one* of the alternatives to the private—there remain of course other alternatives, such as the search for truth, or beauty, or God—disappointment with the pursuit of happiness via consumption activities is likely to redound to the benefit of public action. The extent to which public action is really taken up may well depend on the ready availability or appearance of a "cause": but here we are appealing to exogenous factors which have in principle been ruled out of our story.

Up to this point, I have been trying to make my argument in purely traditional terms. Individuals having had disappointing experiences with one set of activities turn to another set: they *exit* from one to the other. But what about *voice?* It is perhaps time that I made use of my own suggestions for broadening the way in which economists have analyzed consumer discontent and its consequences. In *Exit, Voice, and Loyalty* I argued that the consumer has available to him two main types of activist reactions to discontent. One is *exit,* which is the only response to which economists have paid attention and which they hold to be uniquely effective. This is precisely the reaction of the consumer who, confronted with a disappointing experience in relation to a supplier, looks for a different source of supply, in a competitive environment. So far the argument on reaction to disappointment has been based entirely on this, admittedly powerful, exit mechanism. But disappointed consumers have a very different option that has been neglected by economic analysis: they can raise their *voice,* and thus engage in various actions that range from strictly private complaining (asking for a refund) to public action in the general interest. Whether voice in the latter sense will be generated by any of the disappointing consumption experiences which have been described here will be investigated presently. To the extent that this is the case, the conclusion

---

[2] For an interesting attempt to compare Western and Buddhist "utility functions," see Serge-Christophe Kolm, "La philosophie bouddhiste et les 'hommes économiques,'" *Social Science Information* 18 (1979), 489–588, especially pp. 529–535.

which has been reached so far by the conventional exit route would be *reinforced* by bringing voice into the picture.

Simply in terms of exit-voice theory this is a rather remarkable result. Ordinarily exit means one kind of action and voice quite another, whereas in the case just noted both responses lead to identical kinds of action. The reason is simple: the exit we have been concerned with is exit from the disappointing search for happiness through private consumption, and this exit frequently takes the form of a turn toward public action. In many (though not all) of its manifestations voice is, of course, public action by definition. Therefore, voice reactions that arise from disappointing consumption experiences will reinforce the exit reaction—and the likelihood of a turn toward public action will increase accordingly.

Under what conditions will this reinforcement via voice actually come into play? The question has already begun to be tackled. When the consumers' experiences with the purchase of various services were discussed, it was noted that their disappointment over poorer-than-expected quality could lead to anger at the suppliers. On the other hand, in the case of ineffective psychotherapeutic advice it was argued that consumers may well blame themselves for not being able to take advantage of the services they have received. Furthermore, what sort of action "angry" consumers will take depends, among other factors, on the nature of the defect of the merchandise. If the consumer has just been unlucky and has reason to believe that he has received the one defective specimen, he is likely to turn it in or to ask for a rebate; this is essentially a private response to a private injury. If, however, the consumer finds that the product he has bought is unsafe and that this is a general characteristic of the product, then a public interest is involved, making a public voice response more likely.[3] At the same time, a consumer who has been disappointed in this manner is also more ready than before to question existing social and political arrangements in general. The disappointment he has suffered has itself tendered him, as it were, a *lad-*

[3] See "Exit, Voice, and Loyalty: Further Reflections and a Survey of Recent Contributions" (1974), reprinted in my *Essays in Trespassing,* p. 217.

der which he can use to climb *gradually* out of the private life into the public arena. Later we shall encounter similar ladders that facilitate the move from public life back to purely private concerns—for example, corrupt practices on the part of public officials.

It must be admitted that situations where disappointment with a purchase leads directly and predictably to a voice response are likely to be only a small proportion of the sum total of the disappointment experiences that have been surveyed. Take, for example, consumer durables which generate disappointment because the balance between comfort and pleasure is very different from the one consumers have been used to prior to the advent of durables. These disappointments are not such as to lead directly to some public protest. They are more like the already noted disappointments over ineffective psychotherapeutic services in that no clear remedial or even purely reactive response suggests itself to the disappointed. Such disappointments are diffuse and inchoate, and turn into general frustration and perhaps depression. This mood may of course create in turn a predisposition toward participation in actions designed to effect social and political change. In this indirect way, voice could emerge also from disappointments that do not tender the disappointed that convenient "voice ladder."

Actually, to the extent that the diffuse kind of disappointment prevails, it is difficult to say whether the turn to interest in public affairs that may result is an exit or a voice response. Since exit and voice push in the same direction, there is something of an identification problem here. Both interpretations could be equally plausible and, in fact, both responses may be at work at the same time.

Explaining Changes in Life-Styles: Ideology and Second-Order Volitions

Bringing in voice makes the account of the turn to public action more suggestive than if it ran in terms of exit alone. But has it thereby become wholly compelling? That would be claiming too much. It is still difficult to see how the various rivulets of disappointment that have been identified can merge and develop sufficient force so as to impel an individual to change his "life-style." One way of understanding this mutation is, as was already suggested, to appeal to exogenous events that would help awaken the public citizen who slumbers within the private consumer. But rather than make use of these events to clinch my story I prefer to carry it a bit further under its own steam.

It will be shown in Chapter 8 that the turn from the public back to the private life is often helped along by an *ideology* which proclaims self-interested behavior as a social duty. Accordingly, the dogged pursuit of happiness along the private road is not, as we often tend to think, "what comes naturally"; rather, it is presided over and impelled by an ideology which justifies it, not only in terms of its beneficial results for the individual pursuer, but as the surest and perhaps only way in which the individual can make a contribution to the common good. The ideological claims made for the private life thus sustain the individual's quest with two messages: one, the promise of satisfaction and happiness; and two, the assurance that there is no need for guilt feelings or regrets over the neglect of the public life. These two messages are interrelated so that the experience of disappointment in the pursuit of private happiness directly rehabilitates and reawakens the desire to share in the public life.

Accordingly, the turn to the public life would not come about as a direct result of disappointments over any specific consumption experiences. Rather, these experiences are responsible for the deflation of an ideology that had presided over the quest for private happiness. To the extent that this ideology is resolutely "antipublic," its collapse is likely to lead to a search for meaningful participation in public affairs.

In the preceding account, ideology first buttresses a certain life-style and preference pattern, and then interacts with specific disappointment experiences so as to intensify the resulting changes in preferences. But why should ideology be confined to the role of merely magnifying the oscillations in preferences that originate in the sphere of consumption and consumption-related disappointment? Ideological alienation from "consumerism"—from the quest for happiness via the accumulation of consumer goods—could surely arise ahead of specific disappointment experiences, and the opposite sequence is also eminently realistic. If I have not dealt with such situations, it is because my reasoning has remained anchored in the conventional assumption of economic theory in general, and of consumption theory in particular, which conceives of its central actors as being "decked in the glory of their *one* all-purpose preference ordering," as Amartya Sen put it ironically.[4] My actors shift their preferences or "tastes" as a result of their consumption experiences, but *at any one point of time* they have only a single set of preferences as revealed by their choices and decisions. Since this is still the predominant view, it was just as well to proceed within its framework as far as proved possible. But the task I have set myself—the explanation of large-scale changes in life-style—can be eased by a substantial modification of the conventional postulates, leading to a more complex, but also more plausible, view of the process under study.

The economist's conception of the consumer is simple: the consumer's actual market purchases are taken to reflect a unique preference ordering whose existence is inferred from the observed choices. Should these choices shift, the underlying preferences are assumed to have changed—as a result of what? As already noted, economics is not really much interested in that question. Possible answers—outside of disappointment—range from pure whim or impulse to the decision to give up meat by the new convert to vegetarianism. The illustrations of binary consumer choice situations to be found in the economics literature are often in terms of fairly frivolous alternatives, such as apples vs. pears, or *A*pples vs. *B*lankets—hardly ever in terms of more serious decisions involving

[4] "Rational Fools: A Critique of the Behavioral Foundations of Economic Theory," *Philosophy and Public Affairs* 6 (Summer 1977), 336.

changes in life-style. More attention to the latter kinds of choices and decisions would have suggested that human beings are capable of evaluating and criticizing the entire set of their preferences as "revealed" by their purchases and other actions in terms of alternative sets of preferences; in other words, they can behold several sets of preferences at the same time and then face the problem of deciding which set to live by. In an important and influential article written some ten years ago, the philosopher Harry G. Frankfurt focused on precisely this phenomenon.[5] He made a distinction between *first-order* desires, wants, or volitions which are those that can be "read off" from a person's everyday actions and choices, and *second-order* desires, or *desires about desires,* which will not necessarily coincide with the first-order desires (they will do so only when a person always desires to have exactly those desires which he is expressing through his actions). This "capacity for reflective self-evaluation that is manifested in the formation of the second-order desires"[6] is, according to Frankfurt, peculiarly characteristic of humans, and in his article he proposes, I think persuasively, to *define* a human person as someone who has this capacity to form second-order desires, wants, and volitions.[7]

Those who are capable only of first-order volitions are considered by Frankfurt to be bereft of the human essence. He proposes to designate such impoverished nonpersons by a term that is already in the language, namely, *wanton.* Wantons are totally in the grip of their first-order wants and never step back to criticize or consciously try to modify them. It turns out, then, that consumption theory, one of the most sophisticated branches of economics, has so far dealt exclusively with those infrahuman wantons!

Like "wanton," so is "second-order volitions" an apt term for what has become a topic of increasing interest. While Frankfurt developed his concepts in considering classical

[5] "Freedom of the Will and the Concept of a Person," *Journal of Philosophy* 68 (Jan. 14, 1971), 5–20.

[6] Ibid., p. 7.

[7] His distinctions among these terms are irrelevant for our purpose.

philosophical problems of individual action and free will, Amartya Sen (at about the same time) came upon a very similar idea in connection with the puzzles posed by situations in which self-interested behavior on the part of individuals leads to nonoptimal and even highly undesirable *social* outcomes, as modeled in the famous case of the Prisoners' Dilemma.[8] Sen showed how these outcomes can be avoided if the individuals involved can conceive of several other preference patterns incorporating various degrees of other-regarding behavior *and* if they then so choose among all patterns as to make one of the latter come out on top. He referred to such a choice as a "meta-ranking of preference orderings" (I shall call it "metapreference" for short), a concept that is virtually identical with Frankfurt's second-order volitions. Both concepts encompass what philosophers call weakness of the will or akrasia, which can be defined as a situation in which persons act against their (second-order- or meta-) judgment about the preferred course and are fully aware that they do so.[9]

This whole subject has received considerable attention in recent years because of the importance, for health reasons, of motivating people to stop smoking, or to lose weight, or to exercise, and so on. With the help of our new concepts, such changes in behavior can now be decomposed into two phases: first comes the formation of a new preference for, say, not smoking over smoking as well as of a metapreference for preferring this preference over the one which the agent is cur-

---

[8] "Choice, Orderings, and Morality" in S. Körner, ed., *Practical Reason* (Oxford: Blackwell, 1974), pp. 54–67. See also his "Rational Fools" article, pp. 335–341; and Richard Jeffrey, "Preferences among Preferences," *Journal of Philosophy* 71 (July 18, 1974), 377–392, for an exploration of the topic through formal logic.

There is not much point in attempting to determine who scored a "first" here, Frankfurt or Sen, as the essence of the phenomenon has long been known and was masterfully described in all its complexity by Dostoevsky in his *Notes from the Underground* (1864).

[9] Amélie Rorty, "Self-Deception, Akrasia, and Irrationality," *Social Science Information* 19 (1980), 905–922, and Jon Elster, *Ulysses and the Sirens* (Cambridge: Cambridge University Press, 1979).

rently manifesting. In so doing, that is, by continuing to smoke, the agent now contradicts his newly acquired metapreference; in everyday language, he acts "against his better judgment." The second phase is then the battle actually to impose the metapreference, a battle with oneself that is marked by all kinds of feints, ruses, and strategic devices.[10] This complex two-stage sequence is far more realistic as a description of an important class of behavioral changes than the bland "change in tastes" of conventional consumption theory.

Conversely, the distinction between first- and second-order volitions, or between preferences and metapreferences, is useful primarily in *conjunction with* the analysis of change. If the second-order volitions are permanently in tune with an agent's first-order volitions they merely endorse what the agent is doing already and hardly lead an independent existence. If they are permanently discordant with the agent's choices, then they tend to lose their credibility as being really "there" and will in the longer run be downgraded to "meaningless, hypocritical mutterings and remonstrances." Second-order volitions and metapreferences therefore come into their own in periods of actual, if protracted and tormented, transition from one kind of behavior to another.

In the meantime, it must have become clear that these concepts have an extended ancestry. They are related to Freud's Superego and, reaching much farther back, to the idea of Conscience and of Sinning and Remorse. The tension between what an agent actually does and what he feels he ought to do (or ought to have done) is an important variety of tension between first- and second-order volitions, or between preference and metapreference. But the newer concepts are not nearly as suffused with moralizing as the older ones, such as the "call of conscience," nor do they share in the animosity toward conventional, "repressive" morality that is characteris-

---

[10] See Thomas C. Schelling, "The Intimate Contest for Self-Command," *Public Interest* (Summer 1980), 94–118, and Gordon C. Winston, "Addiction and Backsliding: A Theory of Compulsive Consumption," *Journal of Economic Behavior and Organization* 1 (Dec. 1980), 295–324.

tic of the Superego. Being, or attempting to be, more general, the new concepts are also more versatile, and I shall now show that they have some utility for my present enterprise.

As is well known from works of fiction, a persuasive account of important decisions by individuals to move in a new direction is often produced through the conjunction of preexisting doubts and unease—second-order volitions of sorts—with some catalytic event or experience. Similarly, efforts at disentangling the causes of historically decisive events, such as wars and revolutions, have usually led to a distinction between deep roots or underlying forces and precipitating events. It seems that we cannot really apprehend fundamental change, individual as well as social, without appealing to some combination of both "basic" and "contingent" factors.

There are several reasons for this state of affairs. First of all, the rule in both personal development and social life is reproduction, and any substantial change in course requires an exceptional convergence of numerous favorable conditions such that, looking backward, change looks overdetermined when, in actual fact, every one of these conditions was indispensable for it to occur.[11] Secondly and more fundamentally, the explanation of social change in terms of both underlying forces and precipitating events corresponds to the essence of the human condition—"neither angel nor beast," in Pascal's unequaled formulation. To explain important turns in our lives and societies exclusively in terms of precipitating events would downgrade us to mere playthings of chance; to attribute such turns only to autonomously occurring changes in volitions would on the contrary make us appear as more noble and capable of self-determination than we really are.

Accordingly, any substantial realignment of life-style is best accounted for by a *conjunction* of some preexisting second-order volitions favoring such realignment with an actual precipitating event. More specifically, an agent acquires at one time second-order volitions prodding her to adopt a new pref-

[11] See my essay "The Search for Paradigms as a Hindrance to Understanding," reprinted in *A Bias for Hope,* pp. 358–359.

erence ordering which gives higher marks than at present to involvement in public affairs; after a period of inaction and hesitation, some precipitating event actually makes the agent act in accordance with these second-order volitions. Now, the previously analyzed disappointment experiences—both the more specific ones of Chapter 2 and the more general ones of Chapter 3—fit into this scheme in several ways. Most plausibly perhaps, such experiences can be conceived as distilling, over a period of time, second-order volitions of the anticonsumerism kind, while some exogenous happening (the Vietnam War or some personal neurosis) is the event precipitating the actual turn to public involvement. Alternatively, the disappointment experience could be cast in the role of the precipitating event while the second-order volitions would originate in non-consumption-related experiences, say ideologies implanted in youthful minds about the importance of having a cause or of serving the public weal.

It is now also possible to tackle an important problem in the analysis of disappointment that so far has been left rather in the dark. Common sense and conventional analysis both tell us that disappointment with a given consumption pattern will lead to a change in that pattern "next time," away from the good that is the culprit. But how fundamental or radical is the change going to be? Suppose I am in a restaurant, and am disappointed in the steak I order. Next time, shall I try steak at a different place, or order a different meat dish, or perhaps decide to give up meat altogether? To keep the analysis as simple as possible, it is tempting to assert that the more intense the disappointment, other things being equal, the more radical the response to the disappointment and the shift in preference are likely to be. But one feels instinctively that there is something wrong with such a proposition: no disappointment with a specific meat dish, however severe it may be, can fully explain the decision to become a vegetarian. On the other hand, it is quite conceivable that a specific disappointment, severe *or* mild, is an essential element in a series of reflexive moves that leads up to that radical decision. The question is, in other words, whether the specific disappointment comes at a time when I am ready to take it seriously, a time when it falls on "fertile ground." Such ground consists precisely in second-order volitions or metapreferences manifesting a desire—hitherto ineffectual—to make a radical change in my diet. Similarly, if a consumer-citizen has gradually built up some discontent with his present life-style and feels vaguely that he should devote more of his time and energy to public affairs, then a disappointment with a consumption experience that one was looking forward to—the discovery that "it is not even fun!"—may play a pivotal role in actually bringing about fundamental change.

It is of course conceivable that disappointment experiences are involved in both elements that must come together to produce change. First, such experiences—say, of the more general kind, as noted in Chapter 3—could be responsible for creating, over a period of time, a growing feeling that in pursuing happiness via the accumulation of private goods and pleasures one is barking up the wrong tree. Second, with metapreferences favoring the adoption of a new course thus in place, a specific disappointment experience—say, in relation to some purchase of durables—could then act as the catalytic event for actual change. But there is no need for so stubbornly monistic a conception. My endogenous bias—the determination to explain turns to a new phase as arising exclusively out of the previous one—had the purpose of focusing on certain hitherto neglected aspects of individual and social life. As I said at the outset, I am well aware that nonendogenous factors play important roles in the story I am attempting to tell. If, thanks to the concept of second-order volitions, concrete parts in that story can be assigned to outside as well as to inside factors, so much the better.

The preceding account of the turn to public action requires comment with regard to one of its features that may seem puzzling. Throughout, the turn to public action is taken by people who *have* made new purchases, who have become consumers of automobiles and educational services, rather than by those who have *not* been able to afford them. Are not these have-nots more likely to be aroused? Actually, one of the most solid findings of empirical political science can be called to the rescue at this point: participation in politics is highly correlated with socioeconomic status. But, at the same time, our story suggests a partial reinterpretation of that finding. The traditional explanation has been along the following lines: the more people are endowed with economic and other resources, the more they tend to participate in politics, because these resources make it possible and advisable for them to take an interest in public affairs, alongside their private pursuits, as a smoothly complementary activity. This way of looking at the relationship is implicit in the following summary statement: "the higher-status individual has a greater stake in politics, he has greater skills, more resources, greater awareness of political matters, he is exposed to more communication about politics, he interacts with others who participate."[12] All of this is no doubt true, but perhaps it is not the whole story. Some people with high socioeconomic status may engage in politics because they have become disenchanted with the pursuit of happiness via the private route. Naturally, they do not give up the goods they have acquired as they turn toward the public sphere; but their life now has a new center of gravity and there could be tension rather than harmony between their new avocations and their previous achievements. To look at matters in this way is a far cry from assuming that middle-class people are involved in public affairs only as a natural outgrowth of their success in private life.

It is not at all obvious what kind of public cause will be espoused by those who have been disappointed in the private sphere. But it is a fair inference from our scenario that, in one way or another, they will tend to be reform-minded. Actually,

[12] This is the summary formulation of conventional explanations given by Sidney Verba and Norman H. Nie in *Participation in America: Political Democracy and Social Equality* (New York: Harper and Row, 1972), p. 126. Verba and Nie accept these explanations but provide considerable further analysis, and particularly stress the intervening role of what they call "civic orientation." See also Sidney Verba, Norman H. Nie, and Jae-On Kim, *Participation and Political Equality: A Seven-Nation Comparison* (Cambridge: Cambridge University Press, 1978), for a cross-national analysis of the relationship between socioeconomic status and political participation.

this inference is once again compatible with certain social science propositions. It has long been known that, in the course of economic growth, the upwardly mobile may be less than wholly reliable in their support of the social and political order. This at first sight surprising phenomenon has most commonly been accounted for by the idea of "status inconsistency": while the upwardly mobile rise along one of the dimensions of social status, such as income, a number of rigidities and discriminatory practices block them along other dimensions, so that for a long time they are not fully accepted by traditional elites and consequently may well experience considerable rage and frustration.[13] This explanation of sudden outbreaks of hostility toward the established order on the part of upwardly mobile groups is persuasive in countries where traditional elites are solidly entrenched and are able to brand as a contemptible *nouveau riche* anyone with some economic achievements to his credit. But this is no longer a widely prevailing situation. Our stress on the disappointments suffered by those who accede for the first time to the blessings of new-type consumer goods permits a more straightforward and general understanding of the frequently noted alienation of newly affluent groups from the society in which they have achieved their advances.

There is no implication in what has been said that the *principal* threat to the established social order will necessarily come from those who have suffered disappointment as a result of their purchases. Obviously, there are those who have not been able to make such purchases at all and who may have far more reason to be dissatisfied. Perhaps one can define a revolutionary situation precisely as one in which the dissatisfaction of the have-nots converges with the disappointment of the haves. But speculation along these lines would lead us beyond the boundaries of the present essay.

---

[13] A survey of the sociological literature on this topic will be found in Gino Germani, "Social and Political Consequences of Mobility" in N. Smelser and S. M. Lipset, eds., *Social Structure and Mobility in Development* (Chicago: Aldine, 1966), pp. 371ff.

CHAPTER 5

From Private Concerns into the Public Arena—II

Collective Action and the Rebound Effect

The task of making the turn from private to public pursuits persuasive is not nearly completed. Thus far I have tried to show why the quest for happiness through the accumulation of consumer goods could yield various kinds of disappointments and discontents, making for a readiness to participate more actively than before in public or collective actions of various sorts.

The trouble with accepting this conclusion is that we have been schooled for some time now in the multiple obstacles standing in the way of collective in comparison to individual action. One of these obstacles consists in the possibility that the costs of participation in collective action would exceed the benefits the participating individual could expect to derive from it. This is, for example, said to be the case in elections where the benefit the individual can expect to derive from the marginal efficacy of his vote is small in relation to the cost (primarily in time spent) of voting. This is the so-called voters' paradox—the paradox or puzzle being why so many people bother to vote when they really shouldn't if they were behaving according to the canons of economic rationality. The paradox is not one of the more difficult to resolve, as has been shown by various writers—and as shall indeed be pointed out here also. But I shall first pass on to a more sophisticated argument on the obstacles to collective action. Drawing on the theory of public goods elaborated by a long line of economists from David Hume to Paul Samuelson, Mancur Olson came out in the mid-sixties with a forceful and influential formula-

tion of this matter in his book *The Logic of Collective Action.*[1]
He showed how unlikely it is for individual citizens to participate in collective action even though the benefits of the prospective outcome of that action for the individual might *exceed* the costs of participation. The reason is the famous "free
ride" phenomenon: since the outcome of the collective action
(assuming it is successful) is a public good that can be enjoyed
by all regardless of prior participation, the individual is
tempted to withhold his contribution in the expectation that
others will exert themselves on his behalf. As a result, everyone waits for the next person to jump first—and nothing happens. The only way in which collective action groups such as
public interest associations, unions, political parties, etc. can
build up and maintain a large membership is by distributing,
along with the public goods, some "selective incentives"
which are defined as privately appropriable benefits such as
subscriptions to magazines, insurance services, and so on.

Now it must be recalled that Mancur Olson proclaimed the
impossibility of collective action for large groups (just as
Daniel Bell proclaimed the "end of ideology") at the precise
moment when the Western world was about to be all but en-
gulfed by an unprecedented wave of public movements,
marches, protests, strikes, and ideologies. Olson's book was
widely praised, as indeed it deserved to be for the lucidity of
its analysis, but the inconsistency between the triumphant theory and the recalcitrant practice that followed in its wake has
escaped attention. Here I shall venture a brief aside on the sociology of knowledge. It seems to me paradoxically conceivable that the success of Olson's book *owes* something to its
having been contradicted by the subsequently evolving
events. Once the latter had safely run their course, the many

[1] Harvard University Press, 1965. Some of the subsequent critique of
Olson has been stimulated by Brian Barry's review article of my *Exit,
Voice, and Loyalty* (*British Journal of Political Science* 4 [February 1974],
79–107) where he criticized me for not having adequately appreciated the
force of Olson's argument in relation to my own, particularly with regard
to the prospects for "voice," that is, for private citizens engaging in public
action.

people who found them deeply upsetting could go back to *The Logic of Collective Action* and find in it good and reassuring reasons why those collective actions of the sixties should never have happened in the first place, were perhaps less real than they seemed, and would be most unlikely ever to recur. Thus the book did not suffer from being contradicted by subsequent events; rather, it gained by actively contradicting them and became a great success among those who found these events intolerable and totally aberrant. In this manner, false prophecy can be the foundation stone of fame and reputation in the social sciences!

In contrast to *The Logic of Collective Action*, but aware of its strictures, I am trying to make sense of the periodic outbreaks of mass participation in public affairs and of collective action in general. In this enterprise the vantage point I have reached affords a first argument. A general criticism that can be leveled against the Olson analysis—and against much economic decision theory in general—is that its subjects, while efficient and often even ingenious and devious, are *without a history*. In fact, it is easy to think of situations in which the rule "bygones are bygones"is not likely to be, nor should be, observed. Take first the case where efforts and resources have been poured into policy A rather than B, and where the result, while none too promising, is not yet clearly apparent at the time when a new decision has to be made on whether to spend additional funds on A. Here the decision is likely to be biased in favor of continuing with A, so that, quite possibly, good money will be thrown after bad. Up to a point, this will be done for some quite valid reasons; in certain situations it can be important to maintain self-esteem and to avoid giving the appearance of not being steadfast, especially when outside observers, such as potential adversaries, friends, and allies, are watching.[2] By the same token, once course A has unequivocally proven disastrous, the opposite bias (favoring B over A) is likely to arise, once again for good reasons and in defiance

---

[2] See Charles Wolf, Jr., "The Present Value of the Past," *Journal of Political Economy* 78 (July-August 1970), 783–792.

of the economic theorem according to which "sunk costs" should be disregarded in making choices. This is why we so often overreact to the perceived lessons of history.

Returning to the argument here developed, take a group of people who have experienced a great deal of disappointment in their search for happiness through private consumption: they are infinitely more "ripe" for collective action than a group that is just setting out on that search. It is often possible to explain the choice of an amorous partner that is puzzling to outsiders on the grounds that one (or both) of the persons concerned was "on the rebound" from another involvement that ended unhappily. This sort of "rebound effect" can illuminate many of our social choices. It makes for an exaggeration of the benefits and an underestimate of the costs of the action that provides a counterpoint to the action that has been taken previously and has turned sour. Another way of expressing the matter in the economist's language is to say that once a transaction that one has entered into has turned out badly, a transaction with opposite characteristics may have *negative transaction costs* (alternatively, one might speak of transaction benefits). The transaction will in effect be subsidized—by none other than the transactor himself.[3]

I apologize for using so many words in making plausible something that must seem obvious common sense to the general reader. But as a result of a long process of refinement, economic analysis has moved so far away from common sense that to reestablish contact between economics and common

---

[3] Benefit-cost analysis could of course be reformulated so as to include the rebound effect. The benefit of a certain action B coming after A would then include not only the direct positive consequence of B but also the satisfaction accruing from being no longer involved in action A. But this is of course no longer what is commonly understood by benefit-cost analysis, which would then come to be defined tautologically as a mode of decision-making covering every conceivable human action. For a similar critique of attempts to "broaden" the concept of maximization so as to include any human behavior whatsoever, see Harvey Leibenstein, " 'The Missing Link'—Micro-Micro Theory," *Journal of Economic Literature* 17 (June 1979), 493–496.

sense while still using the concepts of economics is sometimes no simple matter.

Actually the only area in which the "rebound effect" has been given its due in economic writings is in the analysis of migration. Here it was obviously impossible for any realistic description of the process to apply the famous "bygones-are-bygones" rule and to model the decision of the migrant solely on the basis of a cost-benefit calculation relating to the future without taking past experience into account. Hence, migration has long been analyzed in terms of so-called "push" and "pull" factors, with the push factor corresponding roughly to what I have here called rebound effect. It is significant that this account of the migration decision dates from a time when benefit-cost analysis and decision theory were in their infancy and could therefore not choke off a realistic, if unrigorous, treatment of the subject matter.

I submit that a good portion of the so-called puzzle of collective action and participation in public affairs disappears when the rebound effect is taken into account. But by itself this effect only reduces the subjective costs and increases the benefits of any contemplated collective action and therefore does not do away with the logic of the free ride. Also, it may be argued that it is unsatisfactory to have the probability of the turn to public action rest on what are essentially systematic estimating biases and errors on the part of the decision makers. I do not really agree with this objection, for, as already stated, mistake-making is one of the most characteristic of human actions, so that a good portion of the social world becomes unintelligible once it is assumed away.

Be that as it may, the rebound effect is only a partial way of accounting for the turn to public action. There remains the argument of the free ride, that is, the contention that a rational individual, motivated by self-interest, will ordinarily stand on the sidelines and expect others to "do the dirty work" as long as the result of their exertions can be enjoyed by him whether or not he has collaborated in bringing it about. The argument about the rebound effect already casts some doubt on this line of reasoning, for it implies that the satisfaction which disappointed consumers are seeking in turning toward public action derives not just from the expected results of such action. It is precisely this matter that needs to be dealt with at greater length.

Why Free Rides Are Spurned

I briefly return now to Scitovsky's *Joyless Economy* from which I have learned a great deal but which has stimulated me also—as frequently happens—through a number of "intimate disagreements" I have with its argument. In the second part of his book, Scitovsky comments on a number of novelty-intensive and stimulus-producing activities which could provide the pleasures no longer yielded by an environment saturated with identical mass-consumption goods. He comes up with cut flowers for the home, handcrafted goods, and cultural activities such as theater, concertgoing, and the visiting of cafés and bars. With the exception of the last activity, he directs attention to certain kinds of purchases that are based on the stimulation of pleasure through ever new types of private consumption, including the consumption of culture in its infinite varieties. While his critique of American consumption patterns is often acute, the kind of life-style he recommends for maximum satisfaction has a strangely breathless quality: it consists in the relentless search for ever new pleasures and reminds one of the early stage of Faust's compulsive and disastrous quest which Goethe's hero himself characterizes—and deprecates—by exclaiming:

Thus I stagger from desire to rapture,
And in rapture I die of new desire.
(So tauml' ich von Begierde zu Genuss,
und im Genuss verschmacht' ich nach Begierde.)

With their urge to seek out novel "trinkets and baubles" Scitovsky's ideal consumers similarly resemble Don Juan with his never-ending search for sensual-sexual adventures, excitements, and delights. Or, just as Italians under Mussolini were condemned, according to a contemporary quip, to permanent enthusiasm, so are these consumers condemned to permanent pleasure-seeking.

Scitovsky is actually aware that this sort of intense pleasure-seeking is not necessarily everybody's cup of tea, for he speaks at one point admiringly of "people who have one overwhelming passion in life—their work or their hobby—to which they subordinate all else" (p. 75). But he seems to see such people as a tiny elite group and their solution as one that is not available to the great majority. At no point in the book does he deal explicitly with an alternative that is open to the consumer-citizen quite apart from the choice between self-centered comfort and self-centered pleasure: participation in the public life by joining a movement, participating in a community, advocating a cause, etc.

It is both strange and easy to understand why this way out of the frustrations of the purely private and self-centered life should not have been dealt with in Scitovsky's otherwise comprehensive register of consumer choices: strange because the problem of choosing between the private and the public life has been a fundamental theme in Western thought on human conduct from Aristotle and Cicero via Hobbes, Rousseau, Benjamin Constant, and Marx to Hannah Arendt; easy to understand, on the other hand, because a very considerable portion of people's normal activities under modern conditions, during very long periods of their lives, is devoted to their private affairs—so that it *seems* safe to disregard public action and participation as a *real, ever present* potential alternative to private-centered action. The matter is perhaps best illustrated by a joke that was rather current during the "private" fifties. A married woman is asked who makes the decisions in the family and she answers, "My husband, of course, makes the important decisions and I make the unimportant decisions." "So, give me some examples of what's important and what's not." "Well, I decide where we go on our next vacation, whether the children should go to private or public school, whether we should buy a new car or a new house, etc." "And what then are the important decisions that your husband makes?" "Well, he decides what should be done about desegregation in the South, how to handle the conflict in the Middle East, whether we should recognize Red China, etc." In line with the "private" temper of the times, this story ridicules pompous and futile concern with public affairs in contrast to "cultivating one's garden"—but then the sixties came along and demonstrated, with their civil rights marches and the mass protest against the Vietnam war, that, even for a suburban family, the truly important decisions might very well turn out suddenly to be those dealing with public affairs. The joke could simply no longer be told; it had become unintelligible.

Actually, upon looking more closely at Scitovsky's examples of activities particularly rich in "stimulus" and "novelty" rather than comfort, it is possible to discern some elements of public concern and interest. In discussing important differences between patterns of consumption and leisure time uses in various countries, he shows very effectively that the French and English spend considerably more time than North Americans in cafés, pubs, or similar public places. Scitovsky attributes this difference to the greater desire of Europeans for "stimulus" and "novelty." But a different interpretation is possible: in congregating in these public places, the French and English escape from their purely private activities, discuss all kinds of matters of public concern, from current sports and scandals to rising prices and the forthcoming elections, and thereby engage in action that has some bearing on the public interest. In flocking to their cafés and pubs, the French and the English are therefore perhaps not so much manifesting a preference for pleasure over comfort as one for public over private activities. I believe that this is indeed so. But for this belief to carry conviction, the nature of public action and participation, in comparison to private-regarding activity, must be explored in some detail.

One of the major attractions of public action is the exact opposite of the most fundamental characteristic of private pleasures under modern conditions: while the pursuit of the

latter through the production of income (work) is clearly
marked off from the eventual enjoyment of these pleasures,
there is no such clear distinction at all between the pursuit of
the public happiness and the attainment of it. As I have put
the matter on a previous occasion,[4] striving for the public
happiness (in some concrete respect) and attaining it cannot
be neatly separated. Indeed, the very act of going after the
public happiness is often the *next best thing* to actually *having*
that happiness (and sometimes not even the next best thing,
but much the best thing of the whole process, because of the
various disappointments over the results of public-oriented
action—but more about that later).

Public-oriented action belongs, in this as in other respects,
to a group of human activities that includes the search for
community, beauty, knowledge, and salvation. All these activities "carry their own reward," as goes the somewhat trite
phrase, but what really goes on here still needs to be better
understood. To regain a fresh perspective on the matter it is
well, first of all, to cite an observation of Pascal on the nature
of the search for God:

> The hope Christians have to possess an infinite good is
> mixed with actual enjoyment . . . for they are not like
> those who would hope for a kingdom of which they have
> nothing, being subjects; rather, they hope for holiness, for
> freedom from injustice, and they partake of it. (*Pensées,*
> 540, Brunschvicg edition.)

Here the peculiar feature of these activities, that is, the fusion
of—or confusion between—striving and attaining, is particularly well expressed.

Once this essential characteristic of participation in collective action for the public good is understood, the severe limitations of the "economic" view about such participation, and
about the obstacles to it, come immediately into view. The
implication of the confusion between striving and attaining is

---

[4] *Essays in Trespassing,* p. 216.

that the neat distinction between costs and benefits of action in the public interest vanishes, since striving, which should be entered on the cost side, turns out to be part of the benefit.[5]

This is a hard pill to swallow for our imperious bottom-line mentality. For what I am saying is that, at some stage in our cycle, the benefit of collective action for an individual is not the difference between the hoped-for result and the effort furnished by him or her, but the *sum* of these two magnitudes! And a further surprising consequence follows immediately: since the output and objective of collective action are ordinarily a public good available to all, the only way in which an individual can raise the benefit accruing to him from the collective action is by stepping up *his own input*, his effort on behalf of the public policy he espouses. Far from shirking and attempting to get a free ride, a truly maximizing individual will attempt to be as activist as he can manage, within the limits set by his other essential activities and objectives. It is in effect the need to restrain this activism that is at the source of some of the specific disappointments over action in the public interest, as will be shown in the next chapter.

[5] At the outset of his fine study "Two Concepts of Democracy: James and John Stuart Mill," Alan Ryan ventures the same thought by asking: ". . . [with respect to] participation, can we not simply add into our account such previously unthought of benefits as increased self-awareness, perhaps so many of them as to make it no longer a net expense but a net benefit, independently, that is, of its instrumental efficacy?" See Martin Fleisher, ed., *Machiavelli and the Nature of Political Thought* (New York: Atheneum, 1972), p. 80.

A different formulation of the same point is made by James E. Krier and Edmund Ursin in *Pollution and Policy* (Berkeley and Los Angeles: University of California Press, 1977), 270–271. Showing how crises stimulate citizens' protest and thereby lead to policy-making, they note that in these crises citizens view participation no longer merely as an effort, costly in time and money, that is required for the *production* of a desired policy, but rather regard action in the public interest as part of their *consumption*, as directly pleasurable. Similarly, Allen Buchanan in "Revolutionary Motivation and Rationality" in *Philosophy and Public Affairs* 9 (Fall 1979), 71–73, speaks briefly of "in-process benefits" as a possible solution to the public goods problem.

From the point of view adopted here, individuals who have developed a taste for a public good that has yet to be "produced" and who attempt to get a "free ride" by letting others exert themselves on their behalf do not just cheat the community as is implied in the "free ride" metaphor; *they cheat themselves first of all.*

The matter was neatly expressed by Golda Meir in an interview she gave in 1977. She said that life in Israel was so difficult when she first immigrated in 1921 that "people ask me why I came. And I say because I'm selfish . . . when I heard what was being done here I decided that they're not going to do it by themselves. I won't have a share in it? No, I must be a part of it. Just pure selfishness, I suppose. . . ."[6]

My contention that free rides will be spurned in precisely this manner depends crucially on the claim that the confusion between striving and attaining is characteristic, at one stage, of public-regarding activity. That claim can perhaps become more persuasive if it is put into a somewhat different language. For this purpose, it is useful to return to the distinction between comfort and pleasure made in Chapter 2. Comfort is defined as the absence of discomfort—a prime example is the feeling of satiation after the meal. Pleasure is experienced in the process of traveling from discomfort to comfort, that is, during the meal. While language is not totally consistent with this terminology—we speak of eating pleasure, but also of being "pleasantly full"—there is no doubt that the total utility of a meal has these two components, with the pleasure of eating being quite distinct from the comfort of satiation. But then there is yet another stage to be considered. Before the meal, time and effort must be expended on earning the income needed to pay for it: this is the cost to the individual of the ensuing dual benefits of pleasure and comfort. In private consumption activities, the state of satiation or comfort is thus preceded by a time stretch that is divided into a cost segment

---

[6] Marilyn Berger, "Golda Meir Speaks Her Mind," *New York Magazine,* December 12, 1977, p. 12.

(during which income is earned to acquire a good) and a subsequent pleasure segment (during which the good is being gradually appropriated, experienced, and consumed).

What I called the confusion between striving and attaining with respect to public-regarding activities becomes easier to understand with this temporal representation of private consumption. In effect, I affirmed that the neat dividing point between the cost segment and the pleasure segment of presatiation time tends to disappear in the case of public-regarding activities. *Here the pleasure segment penetrates the cost segment and suffuses it with its own experience.* It is easy to visualize such a process which in fact is by no means rigidly confined to public-regarding activities. Even in the process of laboring away at our daily job we do on occasion "savor in advance" certain recurrent private delights that are going to be our reward once the monthly paycheck comes in. But the melting of the cost into the pleasure segment is far more typical of activities that are not concerned with routine private consumption even though they are not necessarily public-regarding. The best illustration is perhaps the phenomenon of *pilgrimage,* which traditionally consists of a lengthy journey to a remote holy site at which prayers are said and other devotional acts performed. "The point of it all is to get out, go forth, to a far holy place approved by all."[7] Obviously, it would make no sense to categorize the travel as the cost of the pilgrimage, and the sojourn and prayers at the holy site as benefit. The discomforts suffered and perils confronted during the trip were part and parcel of the total "liminal" experience sought by the pilgrim, and distance from the site often acted as a stimulant to the decision to go forth rather than as a brake.[8] Close parallels to this aspect of the medieval pilgrimage can be found today, mostly in nonreligious activities. For example, according to a survey of soccer fans in Brazil, attendance of Rio fans at the game is not related to the distance of

---

[7] Victor Turner and Edith Turner, *Image and Pilgrimage in Christian Culture* (New York: Columbia University Press, 1978), p. 7.
[8] Turner and Turner, pp. 7–11.

the fans' homes to the city stadium, again presumably because a true fan considers traveling to the game as part of the fun and of his obligation to the team he is rooting for.[9]

It is not so easy to understand why activities usually considered as costs should become benefits in a different context. One way of approaching this problem is to distinguish between routine and nonroutine undertakings. With regard to routine tasks, there is no doubt in the individual's mind that labor will yield the anticipated outcome—a given job, or an hour of labor, will either yield directly the well-known, sought-after result or entitle the worker to a certain sum of money which can be used for the purchase of a meal or of other desired goods. Under these conditions, the separation of the whole process into means and ends, or costs and benefits, occurs almost spontaneously. In the case of nonroutine activities, such as exertion for a public policy, on the other hand, there is always much uncertainty as to whether the effort will be crowned with success. Strangely, such uncertainty produces not only anxiety. Undertakings that have no precedent and whose successful outcome is not assured are felt as peculiarly noble: effort now becomes "striving," and *as though in compensation for the uncertainty* it is this striving that is endowed with the feeling of already having a pleasurable experience.

But the fusion of striving and attaining that is so characteristic of public action when it is first undertaken can also be explained by two rather less speculative considerations. In the first place, public action is often the result of a radical cognitive change, akin to a revelation. Large numbers of people grow up with the feeling that the existing social and political order is not subject to change or that, in any event, they are powerless to bring such change about. The sudden realization (or illusion) that I can act to change society for the better and, moreover, that I can join other like-minded people to this end is in such conditions pleasurable, in fact intoxicating, in itself.

[9] Janet Lever, *Soccer Madness: Sport's Contribution to Social Integration in Brazil* (to be published by University of Chicago Press, 1982).

To savor that pleasure, society does not have to be actually
changed right away: it is quite enough to act in a variety of
ways *as though* it were possible to promote change.[10] Obviously, if no change is achieved, disappointment will set in.
But that reaction belongs to a later phase of the story.

Secondly, there is the opposite pleasurable experience: not
that *I* can change society, but that my work and activities in
the public arena change and develop *me,* regardless of any
real changes in the state of the world that I might achieve. As
Ryan shows in his already cited study of James and John
Stuart Mill, this was the younger Mill's reason for considering
participation in public affairs as a good in itself, rather than as
a mere means to an end—that was his father's strictly utilitarian view. Participation would "guard against passivity, inertia,
timidity and intellectual stagnation." The open, rather than
secret, vote oddly favored by John Stuart Mill was advocated
by him as one element in an intensive participation that

> involves exposing yourself to new influences, competitive
> views of the world, new demands on your capacities. It
> thus seems quite unlike shopping for policies in your in-
> terest; it is a—on the face of it gruelling—piece of social
> and political education.[11]

The pleasures of political participation come rather hard here,
in typically Victorian fashion. But to the extent that political
activity does lead to self-development—and the twentieth-
century observer must register considerable doubt about the
generality of this experience—it will, in the end, be enjoyable.

The upshot of this discussion is that there is much fulfillment associated with the citizen's exertions for the public
happiness. These exertions are in effect often compared with
the pleasurable experiences of eating and drinking: we speak

[10] See Aristide R. Zolberg, "Moments of Madness," *Politics and Society* (Winter 1972), 183–207. Zolberg defines such moments as those in
which people suddenly feel that "all is possible," and draws for illustrations on various crisis points in the history of modern France from 1848
to 1968.
[11] Ryan, "Two Concepts of Democracy," pp. 104–106.

of citizens "hungering" or "thirsting" for justice,[12] and Tocqueville wrote about the "craving for liberty" that a "few of us" have durably developed.[13] It is in the very struggle for justice and liberty that the thirst is quenched and the craving is gratified. Who, then, would want to miss all that active pleasure and get a free ride to what is at best the comfortable, and usually somewhat disappointing, outcome of these processes? To elect a free ride under the circumstances would be equivalent to declining a delicious meal and to swallow instead a satiation-producing pill that is not even particularly effective!

[12] Pascal speaks of the "hunger for justice" in *Pensées*, 264 (Brunschvicg edition).

[13] The full sentence reads: "What's to be done about it? There just are a few of us stubborn old people who have developed a craving for human liberty . . . and who absolutely cannot give it up." Letter to Gobineau of February 19, 1854, *Oeuvres complètes* (Paris: Gallimard, 1959), Vol. 9, p. 212.

CHAPTER 6

The Frustrations of Participation in Public Life—I

Propelled into the public arena by the disappointments incidental to their earlier concentration on private consumption goals, our citizens are at this point heavily involved in some action in the public interest, spurning, *pace* Olson, any temptation to sit back in the hope of getting a free ride. But the story does not end there. Life in the public arena has a number of disappointments of its own; if they are in turn found to be compelling, the private-public-private story will have been brought close to completion. It may seem that this part is comparatively self-evident, for we are all too familiar with the frustrations that have beset so many attempts to improve the state of the world. Nevertheless, as in the case of the quest for private happiness through the acquisition of worldly goods, this general familiarity has perhaps impeded exploration of processes that are far from transparent.

The following inquiry differs from the previous one. For private consumption pursuits, we began by focusing on the comparative disappointment potential of different large subcategories of purchases, such as durables vs. nondurables, services vs. goods. If the disappointment potential of one of these categories was found to be comparatively high and if this category had lately come to occupy a larger place in total consumer purchases, then it was possible to infer that the private consumption experience as a whole had become more disappointment-prone. It would be conceivable to proceed in a similar way with regard to public action by distinguishing among such categories as community work (P.T.A., etc.), interest group activity, local politics, and national politics. But rather little is known about the comparative importance of these various involvements and particularly about collective shifts, over time, from one kind of involvement to another. Historical observation as well as introspection yield a good deal of knowledge, on the other hand, about some of the principal reasons for disappointment with public pursuits in general, and I shall proceed directly to these reasons. Based as it is on individualistic motives and reactions, a treatment along such lines will have rather little to say of itself about *collective* waves of disaffection with public life occurring in distinct epochs. Such waves can nevertheless be inferred if the prior turn toward public involvements had itself a wavelike character, as has indeed been argued. In this way, a wave of disappointments with the public life can often be understood as the echo and reflection of an earlier collective turn toward public involvements; it will gain in strength and coherence, of course, if disappointments over such involvements can be shown to be systematically generated by institutional features of modern societies, as will in part be argued here.

The Poverty of Our Imagination

An inquiry into why the "public citizen" suffers disappointment can usefully start out with Bernard Shaw's previously cited quip about the two tragedies life has in store for us. One is the nonfulfillment of our desires, the other is—fulfillment. Take nonfulfillment first. Prolonged but largely unsuccessful advocacy of a cause will often bring discouragement and eventual abandonment of a struggle sensed as futile. Another possibility is that nominally success is achieved, but that in triumph the cause turns out to be far less attractive than had been anticipated; in particular, it may acquire a momentum of its own, become "derailed" from the point of view of the early activists, or turn into a real monster as, for example, when it "devours its own children." The result could once again be disillusionment and the consequent withdrawal from the public arena of the original advocates (if they have not been devoured). Yet another reason for withdrawal after success might be that there is no longer any need for action: what is there left to do for a republican after the fall of the monarchy, or for the separatist after successful secession?

In actual fact, however, the decision to give up on public action once one has been drawn into it does not come as easily as a consumer's decision not to return to a restaurant that has proved disappointing. In the case of a movement that threatens to go out of control, participants with a stake in it will close their eyes to this fact for a long time; and once that simply is no longer possible, they may want to make a determined attempt to steady the movement's course before quitting.

Take, on the other hand, a public cause that has failed to achieve its proclaimed objective. Here again, withdrawal is not a foregone conclusion. Most of the time the outcome of public action cannot be unequivocally qualified as either success or failure. The objective of public action is not possession of a commodity such as an apple or a refrigerator about whose nature and uses the customer is fairly well informed, but a "future state of the world" which is expected to be brought about by the adoption of some law or policy, by an election result, or by the overthrow of a hated regime. In other words, the expected result of the public action is a product of the citizen's imagination which is only too likely to be at a considerable remove from the sobering reality that will unfold as a result of the public action. This gap between imagination and reality has been explained by the social need for self-deception, that is, the need to magnify the benefits to be expected from collective action if the considerable exertions required for even modest advances are to be forthcoming.[1] But there is a simpler, less teleological explanation.

The human capacity to imagine social change is notably limited. In most historical societies change has been so slow that the idea of change was not entertained at all. Later, as a result of highly visible, large-scale, and disastrous historical events, such as the fall of the Roman Empire, the idea of *decline* and *corruption* (in the sense of internal deterioration)

[1] Leszek Kolakowski, *Der Mensch ohne Alternative* (Munich: R. Piper, 1961), pp. 127ff.

took shape and dominated thinking about possible directions of change for a long time, up to and including the early Modern Age. Only with the Enlightenment and the French Revolution did the idea take root firmly that society might be changed for the better. But attempts to imagine a better future have remained simplistic and schematic; they usually come up with a state of affairs that is, in some crucial respects, directly *opposite* to the present state, instead of being merely different from it. We may simply be unable to conceive of the strictly limited advances, replete with compromises and concessions to opposing forces, that are the frequent outcomes of actions undertaken under the impulse of some magnificent vision.[2] Given this propensity of the modern imagination to conjure up radical change, and its inability to visualize intermediate outcomes and halfway houses, the results of public action typically fall short of expectations. This is true also for the previously mentioned case of a monarchy that is to be turned into a republic: the *kind* of republic that the republicans are imagining while fighting the monarchy is likely to be a far more ideal state than the one they are actually going to get. We need not worry unduly, so it appears, about the eventuality that no further public cause may be available for espousal after one line of collective action has come to fruition.

It is the poverty of our imagination that paradoxically produces images of "total" change in lieu of more modest expectations. As long as this state of affairs prevails, dissatisfaction with the outcome is a constant companion to action in the public interest. But this dissatisfaction is not in itself a reason why one would necessarily expect a turning away from such action on the part of any but the most naive and weak-willed public citizens. In this respect, dissatisfaction with the outcome of public action is likely to have a rather different sequel from disappointment over a private purchase or consumption act. In the latter case, an exit reaction, that is, an immediate preference shift toward other commodities and pursuits, is normally to be expected. In the case of public action, on the

[2] See also my *Development Projects Observed*, p. 33.

contrary, the partial and incomplete nature of the outcome can be interpreted not only as disappointing, but as encouraging. The fact that there is *unfinished business* left over after every advance could well reenlist the energies of our public citizens and thereby stave off the point in time at which they would want to give higher priority than before to their private pursuits.

Overcommitment and Addiction

There is a need then to probe for more fundamental reasons why people turn away from action in the public interest. Instead of considering only the more or less satisfactory outcome of such action, it will perhaps be more revealing to focus on the nature of public activity regardless of its outcome, on the way it is actually *experienced* and on the possible clash between this experience and expectations.

A very common experience of those who first engage in some public action is that such action takes up much *more time* than was originally expected. One reason for this state of affairs is implicit in what was just said about the poverty of our imagination. If we systematically expect more thorough change to occur than will actually be forthcoming, then, since action takes place in time, it will take more time than was originally allocated to get anywhere close to the desired goal.

This is more than just another facet of the miscalculation about the prospective achievements of public action. The inadequacy of the initially planned effort will become obvious to the actors very soon after it has gotten underway so that pressures will arise to step up the originally planned intensity. In other words, it will soon turn out that action in the public interest takes up *more time per day or week* than had been planned.

Disappointment arises from the disparity between expectations of a pleasurable activity and actual experience. An important dimension of the projected pleasurable activity has to do with its duration. A systematic excess of actual time spent on a given citizen-consumer activity over the time actually budgeted for it can become an important source of disappointment, even though that activity is in itself quite pleasurable. This goes for excessively slow service in restaurants, no matter how good the food, as much as for the discovery that a public cause in which I have taken an interest occupies far more of my time than I had originally contemplated.[3]

An asymmetry between private and public life must be noted here. It is easy for private pursuits almost wholly to fill out our lives and to squeeze out public-regarding activities altogether; this is, in fact, what typically happens a great deal of the time under modern conditions and has been unbeautifully named "privatization." But the opposite process can occur only exceptionally or even not at all if we consider sleeping and "body maintenance" in general as essentially private activities. With public activity being undertaken at the expense of time otherwise devoted to private consumption, and perhaps even encroaching on time normally used for the production of income, the opportunity cost of public activity rises steeply at some point. An underestimate of the time needed for public affairs can therefore be felt as very costly and may then be expected to cause a sharp reaction against the "practice of citizenship."

That participation in public affairs is apt to take too much time under modern conditions has long been an important argument in the debate around the nature of modern democracy. In a critique of Rousseau, who, at least in the *Contrat social*, had urged maximum participation on the classical Athenian model, Benjamin Constant argued in favor of representative rather than mass-participatory politics on the ground that "liberty will be the more precious to us, the more time the exercise of our political rights will leave us for our private interests." Elsewhere in the same speech he explained

---

[3] Disappointment can also result when the time spent on a projected pleasurable activity turns out to be *shorter* than what had been planned. Service in a restaurant can be too rapid—not leaving time for the leisurely conversation around the table which is an important part of a good meal.

that, in modern nations, "every individual is occupied by his speculations, his enterprises, and the pleasures he obtains or hopes for, so that he wishes to be distracted from these matters only for short periods and as infrequently as possible."[4]

Constant pointed to the increased demands on time caused by private activities in the commercial-industrial age. He denounced as unworkable or worse—that is, as potentially despotic—certain forms of government that did not take account of these new realities,[5] and he has turned out to be prophetic. If we stipulate (1) that citizens can spend only a strictly limited portion of their time on public affairs and (2) that they must all be made to participate in major political decisions, then one way of squaring this circle is to have the citizens shout periodically their full, enthusiastic, and unanimous support to The Leader. As is well known, this "time-saving" method of mass participation was developed into a fine art by the most repulsive political regimes of our century.

Constant put the accent on the expansionist tendencies (with regard to time) of private pursuits in the new commercial-industrial age. Actually, Rousseau was not as unaware of these matters as a reading of just the *Contrat social* might suggest. In *Lettres écrites de la montagne,* he speaks of the difficulties of transferring the Athenian model of full-time citizenship to a modern commercial state, even if it be a quasi-city-state such as Geneva.[6] And he makes a particularly striking statement in a fragment entitled "On public happiness" (*Du bonheur public*): "The cause of human misery is the contradiction ... between man and citizen; make man one and you will make him as happy as he can manage to be. Give him wholly to the state or leave him wholly to himself [to his private pursuits], but if you divide his heart you tear it apart."[7]

[4] Benjamin Constant, "De la liberté des Anciens comparée à celle des Modernes" in *Collection complète des ouvrages publiés sur le Gouvernement représentatif ...* (Paris: Bechet, 1820), pp. 209, 249. For a modern treatment, see Robert A. Dahl, *After the Revolution?* (New Haven: Yale University Press, 1970), pp. 40–55.

[5] Stephen T. Holmes, "Aristippus in and out of Athens," *American Political Science Review* 73 (March 1979), 113–128.

[6] *Oeuvres complètes* (Paris: NRF, Pléiade, 1964), Vol. III, p. 881.

[7] *Ibid.,* p. 510.

In a more symmetrical way than Constant, Rousseau here implies that *both* pursuits of happiness, the private and the public, have intrinsically monopolizing ambitions, and that a stable equilibrium between the two is impossible to achieve.

That public activities can encroach unduly on the modern citizen's time is well expressed in Oscar Wilde's objection to socialism. It wouldn't work, he said, because it would take too many evenings.[8] This characteristic formulation goes a bit further than that of Constant in the direction of the line of thought here developed: it suggests a process in the course of which a person would first commit too much time to these activities, only to regret it later.

The simplest explanation of overcommitment (and of the subsequent recoil from it and its cause) is the initial ignorance about the demands public action will make on one's time, in contrast with fairly good information generally available on the time needed for private consumption activities which by nature tend to be repetitive. As I put it some time ago, "time overruns in relation to original estimates and intentions . . . are more likely to occur with respect to the intended 'dashing off' of a letter to the *New York Times* than with respect to the eating of one's breakfast."[9]

Once ignorance is accepted as the principal proximate cause for the overcommitment characteristic of persons who have thrown themselves into some public activity, the question arises why they should systematically *under*estimate the time needed to accomplish their objectives. A number of plausible explanations can be given. First of all, those who take up a new public-regarding activity will often do so under the illusion that it can be accommodated rather easily, without neglecting or sacrificing any of one's usual duties, occupations, and pleasures. Another illusion under which people often labor is that their own point of view makes unique common sense and will easily carry the day. The strength of opposing interests and opinions comes as a surprise. Yet another

---

[8] Quoted in Michael Walzer, *Obligations: Essays on Disobedience, War, and Citizenship* (Cambridge, Mass.: Harvard University Press, 1970), p. 230.

[9] *Essays in Trespassing*, p. 292.

answer lies in the already noted deficiency of our imagination which leads time and again to the setting of utopian goals whose pursuit naturally turns out to be more time-absorbing than expected.

A final reason for overcommitment and the subsequent hostile reaction to it has also been mentioned earlier. Public movements, instead of getting stuck, often develop a momentum of their own and take off in directions unanticipated by the original sponsors and often unwelcome to them. This is the story of most revolutions, but also of other, initially successful movements. In these cases of "loss of control," the original sponsors will strain mightily for a while to correct the course of the movement, and this effort is once again likely to involve them in vast, initially unforeseen expenditures of time and energy.

The time-overrun or overcommitment experience is not the only way in which the subjective reality of public action will differ from what was expected. The actually experienced *quality* of that experience is also likely to have some surprises in store. According to our script, public action is undertaken by the individual as an alternative to the disappointments, the narrowness, and selfishness of the quest for purely private happiness. Action in the public interest is thought of as being infused with idealism, with dedication to a cause, if not with sacrifice for the common good. How surprising it is then to discover, soon enough, that political activity often involves one in a very different set of activities: the making of strange alliances, the concealment of one's real objectives, and the betrayal of yesterday's friends—all of this of course for the sake of the "goal." In other words, the political activist will rediscover for himself the maxims Machiavelli proposed in *The Prince* and the dilemmas Max Weber analyzed in "Politics as a Vocation" and Jean-Paul Sartre in *Dirty Hands*. In the process he may well violate the prevailing ethical code to a far greater extent than he ever dreamt of doing when he was merely pursuing his own personal gain and private consumption goals.

This experience can of course be so dismaying and so contrary to original expectations as to produce an immediate withdrawal from public life. But the opposite reaction is also possible and perhaps more common: a heady feeling of excitement is generated when the consciousness of selflessly acting for the public good is combined with the sensation of being free to overstep the traditional boundaries of moral conduct, a sensation that is closely related to that of power.[10] The totally unanticipated delights (and terrors) of this mixture of experiences are probably an important determinant of the overcommitment already noted. Indeed, they account for more: namely, for the *addiction* to the public life that can often be observed among new recruits to it.

In the present context overcommitment and addiction are obviously related concepts. But there is a distinction. Overcommitment implies that the overshooting of the original time allocation and the consequent squeeze on other activities are *unintended* results of ignorance and estimating errors; the experience of overcommitment immediately detracts from the merits of the activity responsible for it, and some action to cut down on that activity can be expected.

Matters are much more complicated in the case of addiction. Here also the originally assigned limits of involvement are overstepped, but this is so because the new activity is found to be unexpectedly involving. At the level of immediate experience, the squeeze on other activities is fully intended.

As we all know, there are those who never recover from this experience, for whom life without this particular mixture of activities—half delicious, half tragic—is totally without flavor, for whom politics is from then on the "only game in

[10] In a fine analysis of the "problem of dirty hands," Michael Walzer ponders the extent to which political actors suffer, should suffer, or should be made to suffer, for transgressing the moral code in pursuit of "higher" political objectives. See Michael Walzer, "Political Action: The Problem of Dirty Hands," *Philosophy and Public Affairs* 2 (Winter 1973), 160–180. But the political profession is seen in too unattractive a light if the focus is exclusively on situations in which political actors experience the need to make "tragic choices." Such situations are the counterpart of the *power* the politician wields, and the exercise of that power affords an exhilarating experience which the private life cannot hope to match.

town." Others, on the contrary, will resist what they sense as a dangerous activity that is about to "take them over," and a reaction against public activity will set in, just as in the case of unintended overcommitment. The reaction will come, as in other addictions, because people are endowed, as we already know (see Chapter 4), not only with the unique set of preferences of the economics textbook, but with various such sets and also with "second-order volitions" or "metapreferences" which express preferences between these various sets. In the case of addicts, the second-order volition may very well consist in the desire to be rid of the addiction. I have just put matters into the language that Harry Frankfurt and Amartya Sen have devised; that language makes it plausible that, even if the overshooting of the original allocation of time for public activity were the result of a genuine preferential (addictive) choice for some citizens, counter-forces bent on reversing this choice could come into play for a good number of them.

The foregoing account of how the practice of public activity is experienced and how this experience can lead to a retreat from it may seem unnecessarily complex. An alternative, much simpler account is available and has been suggested to me:[11] why not just consider public action as one more activity that will be undertaken until the consumer-citizen has had his fill of it? As a result of gradual satiation (decreasing marginal utility), this activity will then find its proper niche alongside the search for, and practice of, private pleasures. Familiar as it is to those schooled in the gradual equilibrating processes of traditional economics, there is only one trouble with this interpretation: it simply does not mirror what goes on. The turns from the private to the public life and back again are marked by wildly exaggerated expectations, by total infatuation, and by sudden revulsions. It is this reality that I have been trying to picture and comprehend.

[11] By James E. Krier, in personal communication and also in his previously cited book coauthored with E. Ursin, *Pollution and Policy,* p. 280.

CHAPTER 7

The Frustrations of Participation in Public Life—II

Up to now it has been argued that public-regarding activities come to grief because of their intrinsic expansionist ambitions. Straining to occupy a place in individual lives that is vastly in excess of what is tolerable in the longer run, they are sharply cut back, and the chastened "public citizen" reverts to his private affairs. Now I shall try to show that another major strand of disappointment with the public life originates in a very different, almost opposite situation: under modern conditions citizens are subject to strict limits with regard to their involvement in public affairs as certain political institutions keep them from expressing the full intensity of their feelings on these matters. That such forced underinvolvement may resemble overinvolvement in leading to disappointment and frustration is easily understood. A person may well decide that it is not worthwhile to participate at all in a movement if an arbitrary upper limit is set on the contribution he or she is allowed to make.

The Underinvolvement of Voting

To explore this matter I return briefly to what was said in Chapter 5 about the nature of participation in public affairs. Because of the blurring of boundaries between striving and attaining that is characteristic of action in the public interest, it was shown that an individual can actually raise the benefit accruing to him from the public action by stepping up his own input. This is in fact the only way in which an individual can enhance his own benefit because the result of the action, being a public good, is available to everyone. It is thus with respect to those public goods whose pursuit is actively undertaken by an aroused citizenry that Marx's famous rule for production and distribution of private goods under communism, "From each according to his abilities, to each according to his needs," loses its utopian ring. The first part of the rule becomes reality as the public good is being "produced" by the very uneven efforts of differentially motivated citizens, while its second part holds when the public good, having been generated by these efforts, is available for unlimited, noncompetitive consumption so that distribution according to need poses no problem.

Actually, the extent to which this seemingly idyllic situation is realized depends on political conditions. While there are many ways in which an individual can participate in public affairs, the central political institution of modern democracy is the vote. Now the "one man one vote" rule gives everyone a *minimum* share in public decision-making, but it also sets something of a maximum or *ceiling:* for example, it does not permit the citizens to register the widely different intensities with which they hold their respective political convictions and opinions. Political scientists have of course been aware of this fact, but they have primarily examined its bearing on the likelihood that in a democracy minorities that feel very strongly about some issues would come to be systematically and easily oppressed by the majority.[1] The possible boomerang effect of the vote's failure to register intensity of feelings on the vitality of democracy itself has not been noted. Since the point is both unfamiliar and important, it needs to be explained at some length.

If the universal suffrage frustrates the expression of the intensity of citizens' feelings on public issues, the question arises as to what sort of arrangements would afford scope for such expression. A naive device would consist in having voters mark on the ballot or voting machine not only the candidate, party, or policy of their choice, but also the intensity, on some

---

[1] See the discussion in Chapter 4 of Robert A. Dahl's classic essay *A Preface to Democratic Theory* (Chicago: University of Chicago Press, 1956).

numerical scale, with which they wish to register these decisions; and each person's vote would be weighted in accordance with this self-declared intensity. Whether desirable or
not in principle, such a scheme would clearly be unworkable.
With the marking of one's intensity requiring only a few more
seconds' sojourn in the voting booth, most voters would mark
the highest possible point on the intensity scale so as to make
sure that their opinion, however weakly held, will be given
maximum weight when the vote is tallied. People will reveal
their intensities more or less correctly only when they have to
incur some inconvenience for being counted more heavily.
Actually, our present system reflects intensities at least to the
extent that it does not give any weight to the opinions of citizens who feel so weakly about the issues of the day that they
do not undergo the inconvenience of begetting themselves to
the polling station. A more elaborate intensity-revealing system based on the principle of exacting increasing costs for registering increasing intensity is easy to imagine: one might, for
example, permit citizens to vote several times, but only once
each day for a maximum of, say, three days in a row, so that
citizens feeling intensely about an issue could cast up to three
votes, provided they pay the price of returning each of three
days to the voting booth. In such a system each citizen could
decide on a scale of zero to three how strong a message he
wishes to convey.

The point of this still quite fanciful scheme is not to adver-
tise it, but to prepare the ground for a rather surprising assertion: the societies affording the fullest opportunity to express
and signal true intensities are certain repressive regimes in
which all manifestations of criticism, from the mildest to the
most severe, carry some "price tag" in the form of differential
penalties or sanctions. Take, for example, Vichy France during the last year of Nazi occupation. As was memorably
shown in the film *The Sorrow and the Pity,* individual citizens
could here give vent to their political feelings by a wide variety of actions—on the anti-Vichy side, they ranged from the
telling of a political joke as the tamest form of protest to hiding a Jew for one night, and from there all the way to helping
blow up a Nazi troop train as a full-time member of the

maquis. To this scale of possible actions corresponded a scale of sanctions in case one got caught, so that every opponent of the authorities could select the point on the scale that corresponded to the strength of his or her convictions. In this respect, such a regime is better than a well-established democracy at calling forth the full expression of political feelings. This is so not only when a regime has established a wide scale of sanctions for hostile acts of differing seriousness, but also when all such acts are severely punished in principle while in practice the repressive resources of the state are known to be concentrated on detection and punishment of the more serious offenses. Under such conditions there would be widespread participation in (illegal) political activities, all of which would come forward to be gauged (rather than just counted).

The sense of excitement and of participation generated under such conditions contrasts with the boredom and feeling of powerlessness often characteristic of political life in a democracy. This disconcerting finding can in large part be accounted for by the dual character of the vote: on the one hand, it is an essential element in an institutional framework affording a defense against an excessively *repressive* state; on the other, it acts as a safeguard against an excessively *expressive* citizenry. In democratic theory, only the first aspect—the benefit of the vote—has been noted while the second, which is no doubt something of a loss or cost, has been widely overlooked.

Some economists have seen a similarity between voting in a democracy—the election to office of those candidates who have received most votes—and the competitive market process in which consumers distribute their dollars among various goods that are offered at set prices; the term "consumer sovereignty" derives presumably from this comparison with the sovereign voter in a pluralistic polity with universal suffrage.[2] The objections that have been raised against this meta-

[2] Brian Barry, "Does Democracy Cause Inflation? A Study of the Political Ideas of Some Economists," paper to be published by the Brookings Institution in a volume on the Politics and Sociology of Global Inflation, edited by Leon Lindberg and Charles A. Maier, 1979 revision, pp. 23–24.

phor have ordinarily impugned the implicit attempt to let the capitalist market economy bask in the reflected glory of democracy. While this critique is well taken, my objection here is in the reverse direction: in some respects, as will be shown presently, the stress on the similarity between spending one's money on goods and services in the market and casting one's vote on public issues makes the electoral process rather than the market economy appear in too favorable a light.

When competitive markets establish uniform prices for products, one of the positive results is "consumer surplus": that is, every consumer can buy some product at the unique, competitive market price even though the preference of numerous ("inframarginal") consumers for that particular product is of such intensity that they would be willing to pay a higher price. It follows that these consumers are benefited in some sense. Because of the lesser enthusiasm of other ("marginal") consumers for the particular commodity, the market and the uniform price it establishes give (or appear to give) the more enthusiastic ones a "free ride" to the extent of the consumer surplus, that is, to the extent of the difference between what they would have been willing to pay and the actual market price. After our preceding discussion of action in the public interest, it will be clear that this benefit of the market economy does not have a counterpart in the electoral process. True, public issues and candidates for office are subjected to a "market test." But the fact that the enthusiastic partisans of a certain cause or candidate are restricted to one vote each, in just the same way as their most lukewarm supporters, cannot possibly be construed by the former as a benefit or a free ride. On the contrary, they would like nothing better than to be able to express a stronger preference and are prevented from doing so by the "one man, one vote" rule. Consumers' surplus turns here into voters' frustration—a frustration that results from the "rationing" of participation imposed by the central institution of a democratic polity.

Calling attention to this neglected aspect of the vote makes it possible, first of all, to shed some light on the widely noted political apathy characteristic of some well-established democracies. With the vote functioning as the principal instrument

through which most citizens express their political preferences, many of them find it hardly worthwhile to bother with
so watered down a form of participation. There is then indeed
a "voters' paradox," that is, a puzzle why people bother to
vote, but it is very different from the one that has been formu-
lated in cost-benefit terms. The question is why people go to
the polls, considering that they are confined to this tame way
of registering their political preferences: once they find that
they cannot express their feelings about public issues with the
intensity with which they experience them, many are likely to
lose interest in expressing them at all. In other words, it is not
easy to see why this loss of interest should not go all the way,
why it should stop precisely at the level of interest which corresponds to the effort involved in casting a vote, say, once
every four years. In this fashion, political apathy and disappointment with political action are *induced* in a society where
important political decisions can *only* be made by the vote—a
point somewhat reminiscent of Rousseau's famous quip that
the English are free only once every four years when they elect
Parliament. In fact, however, the point I am making is very
different. Rousseau held that the idea of representation and of
periodic election of representatives—an idea he profoundly
disliked—has its origin in the "cooling of the love for one's
country" and in other such unfortunate anticivic develop-
ments.[3] In my argument, cause and effect are reversed, and
the establishment of the vote as sovereign decision-maker
leads to disappointment with the limited opportunities for
civic involvement and hence to its decline. That the periodic
vote is inadequate as an expression of political feelings of high
intensity is clearly shown by the fact that, whenever warm or
hot feelings return, other forms of political action—marches,
demonstrations, strikes, and so on—are rediscovered and re-
sorted to even in democracies.

A distinction could actually be drawn between those
democracies where the vote is widely perceived as the virtually exclusive vehicle for *mass* influence on public policy

[3] *Social Contract,* Book III, Chap. XV.

and others where, in addition to the vote, a variety of more direct and expressive forms of mass participation still play a potentially important role. The distinction has a bearing on the character of parties: where the vote is paramount, as in the United States, parties are likely to become activated primarily at election time; when, for historical and other reasons, the vote has not achieved undisputed supremacy, as in France, parties are more likely to function on a permanent basis as focal points for possible mobilization of their members and sympathizers *at any time.* Differences in the degree of participation in elections may be related to this distinction. Turnout is likely to be higher when parties are permanently calling citizens' attention to various public issues than when they attempt to arouse the voters just at election time. Hence, paradoxically, a generalized belief that "electoral politics are the only politics" may contribute to a low turnout. Perhaps the high rate of abstentions in the United States, in comparison with Continental Europe, can be partly explained on these grounds.

When mass actions are no longer forthcoming, there may of course still be individuals who feel so strongly about certain issues that they are unwilling to abide by the limitation on "expressiveness" implicit in the vote. Terrorist actions of the few thus provide the counterpart of apathy of the many in a number of modern democracies; both are reactions to the limitation on political participation imposed by democratic institutions.

Some qualifying remarks are in order. First of all, I must reassure the reader that I am aware of the manifold forms other than the vote which political participation can take, as well as of the important research that has been published on this very topic during the last ten years, particularly by Sidney Verba and his collaborators.[4] The other-than-vote forms of

___

[4] See Sidney Verba and Norman H. Nie, *Participation in America* (New York: Harper and Row, 1972) and Sidney Verba, Norman H. Nie, and Jae-On Kim, *Participation and Political Equality: A Seven-Nation Comparison* (Cambridge: Cambridge University Press, 1978). An early large-scale study is Lester Milbrath, *Political Participation* (Chicago: Uni-

political participation include two principal categories: (1) attempts at influencing the vote, such as attending meetings as a partisan, contributing funds, working actively in the campaign, etc. and (2) attempts at influencing public policy directly by taking an interest in community activities or national problems, generally by participation in voluntary groups and organizations.

The first category no doubt makes it possible for large numbers to participate in politics at certain times at a feverish pace, but this activity labors under two limitations. In the first place, the "campaign workers" exert themselves only at election time, that is, at stated, fairly distant time intervals, no matter how strongly they may feel about public affairs in between elections. Second, they are at several removes from the real policy-making that is presumably of primary interest to them: they try to convince other voters to cast their vote for a person who will then make policy, instead of applying pressure toward adopting or reversing a policy through more direct action. A political activity that has so indirect and tenuous a connection with the real change political activists want to bring about is therefore unlikely to retain its grip on the participants *unless* they are afforded occasional opportunities for actions of a more direct kind, outside of the electoral calendar. Once again if "electoral politics is the only politics," the vigor not only of the voters, but even more of the campaign workers, is likely to flag.

This brings me to the second category of political participation other than the vote, that is, to the attempt at influencing policy directly by bringing pressure of public opinion to bear on government, local and national. Such pressure is generated by joining with like-minded citizens in associations, coalitions, pressure groups, and lobbies of various kinds. The appearance of numerous movements and organizations of this

---

versity of Chicago Press, 1965). For an incisive critique of the approach to the study of participation on the part of mainstream American political science, see Alessandro Pizzorno, "An Introduction to the Theory of Political Participation," *Social Science Information* 9 (Oct. 1970), 29–61.

sort—from proenvironment groups to Common Cause, from Right-to-Life to the consumer movement—can actually be taken as a confirmation of my thesis on the underinvolvement of voting. Because many citizens come to regard the vote as an inadequate way of expressing their strong feelings, they eventually find and invent other forms of venting those feelings and of exerting influence.

It can even be argued that the experience of underinvolvement, which is consequent upon modern democratic institutions, carries some responsibility for the rise of the "single-issue interest group," that worrisome contemporary phenomenon. Anyone who is willing to judge politicians exclusively in accordance with their stand on one, highly specialized issue, such as opposition to gun control, must have remarkably strong feelings on that issue. The simple act of joining such a single-issue movement therefore expresses high intensity of feelings and may be engaged in *for that very reason* by the person who feels frustrated by the ceiling on participation implicit in the vote. In other words, it is possible that people join these movements not so much because they believe in the overriding importance of the particular issue, as because they want to make manifest, to the world, their friends, and themselves, that they are able to work up very strong feelings about *some* public issue. In this manner, a political system in which electoral politics is supposed to be the only politics can engender quite another kind of politics that carries a new, insidious menace to the proper functioning of democracy.

In the long run, however, the existence, busyness, and occasional effectiveness of the various interest groups and movements cannot hide the fact that the basic political direction of a democratic country results from the vote, that is, from a method of aggregating preferences that places a ceiling on citizens' involvement. This ceiling is a necessary, integral, and central part of the democratic process. It also limits the exercise of the political passion in such a way that disappointment is generated and depolitization may result.

A Historical Digression on
the Origins of Universal Suffrage

This matter leads me into a brief digression, in the form of a historical speculation. As is well known, the first nationwide election under universal direct suffrage (for males) was held in France, in April 1848. The decision taken by the Provisional Government on the morrow of the February Revolution has often been hailed as a historical breakthrough and as one of the few real concessions then made to popular forces. Every Frenchman of age was given the right to vote when the most liberal European countries of the time made the franchise depend on rank and wealth and while even in the United States a number of restrictions prevailed, quite apart from slavery.[5] Remarkable as that decision was, hindsight suggests a rather different interpretation: when the vote was granted to the people of France, and in particular to that obstreperous, unruly, and impulsive people of Paris which had just made the third revolution in two generations, it became enthroned in effect as the *only* legitimate form of expressing political opinions. In other words, the vote represented a new right of the people, but it also restricted its participation in politics to this particular *and comparatively harmless* form. It was similarly a means of offsetting the perpetual Parisian avant-garde and direct-action leanings by the much more traditional and law-abiding mood of the provinces. This interpretation of the universal vote decision as restraining and conservative in fact though not, of course, in intent is suggested by the conservative outcome of the April 1848 elections to the Constituent National Assembly—and, more important, by the moral force and claim to legitimacy which this freshly elected body was able to throw against the insurgents of June 1848.[6]

[5] Roger Price, ed., *1848 in France* (Ithaca: Cornell University Press, 1975), p. 28.

[6] In spite of the conservative outcome of the April 1848 elections, subsequent by-elections so frightened the conservative government of 1850 that in May it decreed residence and other requirements for voting and

If insurrection is justified in the *absence* of free and general elections, as republican opinion maintained at the time, then, in counterpart, the implantation of universal suffrage could be held to be an antidote to revolutionary change. This was indeed the way the more conservative republicans saw it soon after the February Revolution, and the idea is well expressed in the contemporary slogan, "the universal suffrage closes the era of revolutions." All of this is perfectly illustrated in an 1848 engraving (see next page) showing a Parisian worker in a perplexed and even distraught mood as he discards his rifle for a ballot he is about to drop into an urn labeled "suffrage universel."[7]

The advantages of this kind of deal were later stressed by Gambetta, the fiery orator and "father of the Third Republic." Universal suffrage had been reestablished by the constitution of 1875, but the young Republic was threatened in 1877 by the authoritarian tendencies of General MacMahon, who had been appointed President for seven years in 1873. A few days before the elections that were to turn into a resounding defeat for the General, Gambetta implored particularly conservative opinion to stand by universal suffrage:

> I speak to those among the conservatives who have some concern for stability, some concern for legality, some concern for moderation . . . in public life. To them I say: How could you not see that with universal suffrage, provided you let it function freely and respect, once it has spoken, its independence and the authority of its deci-

---

thereby indirectly disenfranchised primarily some of the poorer sections of the population. These restrictions were then lifted in a shrewd move by Louis-Napoléon for the purpose of the plebiscite of December 1851. See Maurice Agulhon, *1848 ou l'apprentissage de la république, 1848-1852* (Paris: Seuil, 1973), pp. 149–151, and Roger Price, *The French Second Republic* (London: B. T. Batsford, 1972), pp. 258–260, 322.

[7] Also reproduced in Maurice Agulhon, *Les Quarante-Huitards* (Paris: Gallimard/Juillard, 1975), illustrated page 5. The slogan and the to-be-cited Gambetta speech were brought to my attention by Raymond Huard, of the University of Montpellier, who is writing on the history of the suffrage in nineteenth-century France.

(Bibliothèque Nationale, Cabinet des Estampes.)

As universal manhood suffrage is established in France after the 1848 Revolution, a Parisian worker gives up the bullet for the ballot, with qualms.

sions—how could you fail to see, so I ask, that you have
here a means of ending all conflicts peacefully, and of
solving all crises? How could you fail to understand that,
if the universal suffrage functions in the fullness of its
sovereignty, *revolution is no longer possible* because revolution can no longer be attempted and that a coup d'Etat
need no longer be feared when France has spoken? (Very
good! Very good! —Applause)[8]

Here, in a beautiful rhetorical flourish, is the point I have been
making.

The argument was not voiced in France alone. Even though
the English had been spared what they liked to call the "con-
vulsions" of their French neighbor, concern about popular
upheaval was a constant theme in the discussions on political
and electoral reform throughout the nineteenth century. In
the debate on the Second Reform Bill of 1867, which for the
first time extended the franchise to significant groups of workers and other lower-income people, Leslie Stephen, the critic,
essayist, and historian of ideas, wrote in favor of reform rather
along the lines of Gambetta. In England, of course, he had to
argue, not that revolutions would no longer occur *with* the extended suffrage, but, somewhat more imaginatively, that they
were threatening *without* it:

... how far is the remedy of excluding [the working]
classes from any solid share of influence sound or satisfactory? Does not the fact of excluding them from legisla-
tive influence, teach them to look to other means ... ? We
have constantly had the tyrannical practices of Trade
Unions dinned into our ears, as though they supplied a
conclusive reason against allowing workmen to have the
suffrage. To me, it seems equally conclusive the other
way.... [T]he exclusion of workmen from the franchise
tends, if anything, to spread [Trade Unions] faster; if men

[8] Speech of October 9, 1877, in *Discours et plaidoyers politiques de M.
Gambetta,* edited by Joseph Reinach (Paris: Charpentier, 1882), Vol. VII,
pp. 282–283. My emphasis.

have no chance of receiving help from Government, they
will look to themselves, and no one can blame them. . . .
The plan of remedying an evil by ignoring it is radi-
cally bad and short-sighted. It tends directly and energet-
ically to increase that profound division of classes which
is one of the great evils of the time, and which may some
day result in the very catastrophe most dreaded.

The author also argued that, once in Parliament, that is,
"out in the open," the workers' representatives would become
domesticated and even, he hoped, divided:

Doubtless Members of Parliament would have to discuss
more questions affecting the social welfare of their coun-
trymen than they do now; and that is one of the paramount reasons for Reform: but it is quite another question whether workmen would be able to enforce unfair
demands better in Parliament than out of it. Many excellent reasons may be given against it. They would have to
discuss these questions before the whole nation, instead
of fighting in the dark; the whole intelligence of the country would be brought to bear upon their claims and detect
their unsoundness: the mere putting them into shape and
discussing them would infallibly bring out the differences
among the workmen themselves.[9]

Here, then, is another cogent argument for the suffrage as a
means of taming revolutionary energies and of setting limits
to both participation and influence of the emergent masses.

It is perhaps this historical background to the establishment
of universal suffrage that is at the origin of the since then so
frequently voiced criticism of "formal, bourgeois democracy."
A traditional argument here has run as follows: with *economic*
power being distributed quite unequally, voters will be subjected to direct pressures of landlords and other such bosses;

[9] Leslie Stephen, "On the Choice of Representatives by Popular Con-
stituencies" in George C. Brodrick *et al., Essays on Reform* (London:
Macmillan, 1867), pp. 121–123. This is a collection of proreform essays
by various prominent persons, almost all from Oxford and Cambridge.

even when the vote is secret, voters will come under the influence of the bourgeois-dominated press and other media; therefore, the electoral cards are inevitably stacked against the Left and progressive social change. But on the basis of the preceding considerations it is possible to conjecture that a more fundamental reason for the antagonism to "formal" democracy was hostility to the vote as a false gift, a hostility born of the feeling that the resolute opponents of the existing social and political order had been tricked into a poor bargain: the vote was a mess of pottage for which they had inadvertently bartered away their birthright, Lockeian or otherwise, that is, the right to give vent to their discontent by any means whatsoever, including that of fomenting insurrection, subject only to the intensity of their own feelings. The trouble with the vote, in other words, is not so much that the outcome of voting is stacked, because of the way in which economic and political power is distributed in society; rather, it is that the vote *delegitimizes* more direct, intense, and "expressive" forms of political action that are both more effective and more satisfying.

The gradual establishment of universal suffrage in Western Europe and the United States went hand in hand with the transition from the open to the secret vote. There were of course good reasons for this conjunction: as poorer and socially subordinate strata of the population acceded to the vote, it became more important than at earlier times, when only the propertied elite voted, to guard against vote-buying by the rich and against intimidation and reprisals by the powerful. But, as will be shown in a forthcoming study, the establishment of the secret vote also meant the loss of considerable opportunities for public display of public spirit and participatory energies; and it was opposed, for that reason, by some leading progressive figures of the day, such as John Stuart Mill.[10] Prior to the secret vote, elections were boisterous celebrations; they tended to become much tamer once the vote had been

[10] I am referring to research by Andreas Teuber. For a very brief and preliminary summary, see his Op-Ed article, "Elections of Yore," in the *New York Times* of November 4, 1980.

turned into a private, almost introverted affair. Essential as it became with the extension of the franchise, the secret vote compounded the very loss of opportunities for expressive forms of political action that the franchise itself entailed.

My argument should not be misunderstood. It could be taken as a lament over some marvelous, fully expressive, and ideally participatory polity that we have lost because of the institution of the universal secret vote. I must therefore be quite clear and point out that to my knowledge no such golden age ever existed; it is simply that the considerable advance implicit in the establishment of the universal, secret suffrage came at a cost that has gotten lost from view. Moreover, I hold that the cost is unavoidable in the context of the vote. In other words, that cost cannot be significantly reduced by tinkering with the way in which the vote is organized, but only by tolerating or fostering other meaningful outlets for more intensive participation in public affairs.

The reason that intensity of feeling or commitment cannot be revealed and made to count in connection with the vote has already been noted. Because of strategic considerations, individuals would tend to *overstate* their intensity if there were some voting mechanism that would give a greater weight to intensely held opinions. Furthermore and more important, even if it were possible to devise a voting system that would successfully reveal everyone's truly held intensities, it would be *undesirable* to have the vote reflect such intensities. The basic reason for limiting citizens to a binary expression of their preferences, such as yes-no or for-against, is, of course, the democratic postulate of equality.[11] Another possible,

---

[11] See Dahl, *Preface,* p. 90. A system that would respect the postulate of equality, while still revealing intensities to a certain extent, is the so-called "single-transferable vote," proposed in the nineteenth century by Thomas Hare (also called sometimes the Hare system of proportional representation). In this system voters indicate on their ballots their order of preference for all the contending candidates (or parties). The outcome reflects individual intensities of like or dislike more than the normal method of casting a vote solely for the preferred candidate, *provided* there are more than two candidates or parties. Perhaps it was also for this

though less convincing, reason is the same sort of paternalistic concern of the state for the welfare and sanity of excessively impulsive, would-be self-immolating and similarly unstable citizens that makes for a rigid ceiling on the amount of blood any one individual may supply to a blood bank. As it has evolved, the universal vote is an institution that is both indispensable and hard to improve upon, except for devices designed to make it ever more universal and accessible. Just for that reason it is important to realize the inevitable liabilities which it entails and on which I have dwelt here.

The arguments of this and the preceding chapter on the recoil from involvement in public affairs have been very different, even contradictory, so it is well to draw them briefly together and to attempt a reconciliation between the two principal lines of thought that have been developed. I have tried to go beyond some of the more obvious reasons why action in the public interest meets with disappointment, and have focused on two opposite consequences or attributes of that action: overcommitment, on the one hand, and underinvolvement, insofar as political action is essentially limited to the vote, on the other. In short, the trouble with political life is that it is either too absorbing or too tame. It could of course hardly be criticized on *both* these counts by the same public actor at one point of time. But the apparent contradiction vanishes once we allow for different groups of political actors that could go through either one or the other of the two disap-

---

reason that John Stuart Mill was so enthusiastic a partisan of the Hare system, as discussed in Dennis F. Thompson, *John Stuart Mill and Representative Government* (Princeton: Princeton University Press, 1976), pp. 101–112. The principal reason that the Hare system has made few converts is its complexity. This drawback is still more pronounced in the case of "point voting," an ingenious proposal specifically designed to solve the intensity problem. The proposal was pioneered by Richard Musgrave, and a full treatment is in Dennis C. Mueller, Robert D. Tollison, and Thomas D. Willett, "Solving the Intensity Problem in Representative Democracy," in R. C. Amacher, R. D. Tollison, and T. D. Willett, eds., *The Economic Approach to Public Policy* (Ithaca: Cornell University Press, 1976), pp. 444–473.

pointing experiences. It has not been mentioned so far that a certain type of *active* participation in politics requires not only the *willingness* to participate but also certain kinds of *abilities,* such as a talent for dealing with people or for speaking in public, and in general what has been called "subjective political competence,"[12] so that not everybody who is caught by the public interest is subject to all of its absorbing temptations. It is therefore quite conceivable that different members and groups of the same society typically go through two opposite, but similarly disappointing experiences when they become more open to involvement in public affairs: those who are capable of participating actively in the shaping of events may then experience the perils of overinvolvement, while those who want to do no more *but also no less* than forcefully register their aroused feelings on this or that issue may suffer from underinvolvement once they realize that they are essentially limited to the vote. In addition, it is possible for both phenomena to be experienced by the same person at different periods of his or her life; more interestingly, a person could realize—and I think this is a rather frequent intuition—that *participation in public life offers only this unsatisfactory too-much-or-too-little choice and is therefore bound to be disappointing in one way or another.*

[12] See Gabriel A. Almond and Sidney Verba, *The Civic Culture* (Princeton: Princeton University Press, 1963).

CHAPTER 8

Privatization

Our inquiry began with the consumer-citizen concentrating single-mindedly on his private welfare. We have followed him on a long and roundabout voyage and he is now at the stage where participation in public affairs no longer seems as attractive as it once did. To get back to the point of departure—with the voyage presumably starting all over again—only one step remains to be taken and accounted for: the withdrawal to the private sphere following upon disappointment with the public life.

As was noted at the outset of Chapter 6, this movement seems rather unproblematic in comparison with its opposite, the turn from the private to the public: one reason is no doubt that it involves only individual rather than collective action. The difficulties of the latter have been so much pondered over that the modern observer fully expects the plunge into public action, widely sensed as difficult-to-understand, half-irrational, and therefore somewhat censurable behavior, to be promptly followed by a return to "normalcy": that is, to the pursuit of the private rather than the public happiness. It is just possible, of course, that this view of the matter is biased by the ideological forces impinging upon the observer in our privatized society. Citizens of an earlier age, brought up according to a code of values stressing the civic virtues, may very well have experienced difficulties in accounting for a turn from the public to the private sphere even greater than those of modern observers chafing under the task of explaining a movement in the opposite direction. After all, the original meaning of *private,* current in the fifteenth and sixteenth centuries, was, according to the *Oxford English Dictionary,* "not holding public office or official position." The term stems indeed from the Latin *privare,* that is, to deprive or to bereave. The original meaning survives today in the army "private," that is, the "ordinary soldier without any rank or position" (*OED*). Thus a private man used to be found at the lowest end of the social scale. For women, on the other hand, the ranking was reversed, inasmuch as a *fille publique* or "public woman" has long been one of the many synonyms for a prostitute. Taboo for women, the public arena was where men belonged and acquired distinction.[1]

Historically, then, privatization is anything but an obvious process. We are in fact only beginning to understand—as Quentin Skinner has pointed out to me—how the Renaissance stress on civic virtue and involvement in public affairs gave way, in the course of the following three centuries, to the idea that pursuit of private self-interest is most conducive to a well-regulated social order. Even toward the end of that process, in the eighteenth century, a term such as "happiness," which is today almost wholly relegated to the private sphere, still had a substantial public dimension. When Jefferson, in the Declaration of Independence, designated the "pursuit of happiness" as an inalienable right, he had in mind the *public* happiness, that is, a performance of economy and society that is satisfactory to its members.[2] In eighteenth-century Italy and France, likewise, *felicità pubblica* and *bonheur public* were common concepts, standing for the well-being of the community. To give just one example: Turgot used the term "la science du bonheur public" (the science of public happiness) to stand for the branch of knowledge that was then becoming known as political economy and later turned into economics—unfortunately, that sanguine paraphrase was to be decisively superseded by Carlyle's "the dismal science"![3]

---

[1] For the traditional relegation of women to the private realm, see Michelle Zimbalist Rosaldo, "Women, Culture and Society: A Theoretical Overview" in M. Z. Rosaldo and L. Lamphere, *Women, Culture, and Society* (Stanford: Stanford University Press, 1974), pp. 23ff. and Jean Bethke Elshtain, *Public Man, Private Woman* (Princeton: Princeton University Press, 1981).

[2] See Garry Wills, *Inventing America: Jefferson's Declaration of Independence* (Garden City, N.Y.: Doubleday, 1978), Chaps. 10 and 18.

[3] See Turgot's commentary on Richard Price's *Observations on the Importance of the French Revolution* in a letter to Price of March 22, 1778, in *Oeuvres* (Paris: Delance, 1810), Vol. IX, p. 377.

Later in this chapter, some comments will be offered on the ideological props of the major public-to-private transition that took place in the early modern age. But even from today's perspective, at least one aspect of such transitions is not at all obvious. Why should public pursuits, once they have given rise to disappointment, be so often given up *altogether* for that overwhelming concentration on private affairs with which our story started out? As was noted before, we have here a real asymmetry, as a similar concentration on public affairs at the expense of private life hardly ever occurs and can even be considered a physiological impossibility (see p. 97). According to the economic reasoning which has served as basic supporting structure for our whole argument, disappointment with an article or activity would be expected to lead to reallocation: in the next period, less money will be spent on the article and less time devoted to the activity. But why should the article or activity be virtually given up? Under modern conditions (this qualifying clause is important) the taste for public affairs appears to be subject to a special kind of instability whose nature needs to be understood. In this endeavor, the marginal adjustments characteristic of economic processes must be supplemented by some institutional, ideological, and psychological mechanisms that account for the speed and thoroughness of the public-to-private transition.

Corruption

One such mechanism is corruption. Ordinarily the analysis of corruption has proceeded through an examination of the economic institutions that make corruption possible: for example, allocation of goods and services through the market makes for fewer opportunities for corruption than an allocation mechanism that depends on administrative decisions. In other words, corruption has been studied primarily by asking questions about the supply of the opportunities for corruption.[4] While the supply side is obviously important, the actual

---

[4] See, for example, Susan Rose-Ackerman, *Corruption: A Study in Political Economy* (New York: Academic Press, 1978).

incidence of corrupt behavior will also depend on how many individuals with access to the opportunities are corruption-prone rather than corruption-averse. Now the ratio of the latter to the former is likely to fluctuate in line with what is known as "public morality" or "public spirit," and in many countries corruption seems to vary at least as much with changes in this "demand" factor as with changes in the institutional framework which spells out, on the supply side, the opportunities for corruption. It is therefore important to get a handle on the demand side.

The public-to-private transition that is being described here provides one such handle. Take a person who has been heavily involved in public affairs and, as a result, holds some public office, but has now become disappointed for one reason or another: one way in which he can respond to his new set of private vs. public preferences is by taking a bribe. What has been called the "unblushing confusion of the business of government with the promotion of private fortune"[5] often occurs after the first flush of enthusiasm for public service has given way to a more jaundiced assessment of the prospects for improvements in the public happiness. It is at such moments that opportunities for personal enrichment at public expense on the part of those who have successfully taken a particularly strong interest in public affairs are apt to be perceived and seized. Corruption can thus be viewed as a response to a change in tastes: losses in the satisfaction that is yielded by action in the public interest are made up by material gains. But ordinarily the process is not one of small, optimizing, public-private adjustments following upon small variations in individual preferences. This is so because the *practice* of corruption has a further powerful effect on public-private preferences. If I act this way, so the erstwhile public citizen will argue in order to justify his corrupt actions to himself, then the public cause on which I had set my hopes must really have taken an abject turn. In this manner, corruption which is at

---

[5] L. H. Jenks, *The Migration of British Capital to 1875* (London: Jonathan Cape, n.d.), p. 63.

first a response to dissatisfaction with public affairs becomes a determinant of further, more profound disaffection which in turn sets the stage for more corruption. At the end of the process the public spirit is driven out altogether.

This cumulative dynamic is not likely to operate with equal force under all circumstances. It thrives particularly in an ideological ambience where the private and the public spheres have come to be sensed as strictly separate and even opposite, so that any blurring of the confines seems incongruous or immoral. This ambience is on the whole restricted to certain Western societies which have passed through a period characterized by a nearly total separation of the day-to-day workings of the economy from state control. The "unblushing confusion" of the public and private spheres, which was given quite properly the more neutral term "patrimonialism" by Max Weber, prevailed in most countries up to the nineteenth century and is still today in evidence over broad areas of the globe. There was in fact a long period during which the only, or the most expeditious, road to wealth was by way of political power and public office; under those conditions people obviously do not wait until they are disappointed with the public sphere to lay aside a nest egg or two. Private enrichment and the feeling of laboring for the public good can here coexist so that the practice of what today is called corruption would not undermine the satisfactions of "public service"; rather it would nicely supplement them.

Nevertheless, the separation of the two spheres has been proclaimed in the West, and it has become an aspiration elsewhere as well. Under those conditions, corruption can provide the "public citizen" with a rapid transition back to exclusively private concerns.

Public Virtue Debunked

The retreat from the public life is not likely to be a gradual and limited affair for other, more general reasons. They are connected with the very manner in which action in the public interest was originally taken up. The principal characteristic of that action, it will be recalled, was the fusion of striving and attaining as a result of which striving, that is, participation in public action and its cost to the individual, was in effect transformed into a benefit. The scales were tipped decisively in favor of public action by this strange mutation which has, however, a counterpart: when disappointment with public action sets in, the spell that transformed costs into benefits will be broken and the more usual kind of cost accounting will reassert itself. Along with openings for corruption, opportunities for free rides will suddenly seem attractive. As a result, the citizen will feel that he has vastly and unnecessarily overextended himself into the public domain and that a ruthless cutting down on those commitments is in order.

This built-in instability of the proclivity toward public action has an ideological counterpart. After a long immersion in purely private concerns, the discovery of action directed to a public purpose constitutes a liberating experience, "a way of rising above the self-seeking of the individual and the family," as Jacob Burckhardt put it.[6] The greatest asset of public action is its ability to satisfy vaguely felt needs for higher purpose and meaning in the lives of men and women, specially of course in an age in which religious fervor is at a low ebb in many countries.

But the solidity of this asset is by no means assured. Just as public action can forfeit the privilege of having its costs computed as benefits, so can it lose its reputation as a principal outlet for man's higher impulses. Standing on so high a pedestal public action is exposed to the possibility of resounding downfalls. This is what happened in the seventeenth century when a sharp and concerted attack was staged on glory and glory-seeking, that is, on what had been proclaimed as the highest type of human behavior in the late Middle Ages and particularly the Renaissance. This still insufficiently understood intellectual movement has been aptly called "The Dem-

[6] In *Force and Freedom: Reflections on History* (New York: Pantheon, 1943), p. 118.

olition of the Hero."[7] Its most telling point was the suggestion that the abnegation and dedication to higher causes allegedly characteristic of glory-seeking were smokescreens for self-love and self-promotion. The same suspicion of the motives of those who take a public cause to heart was often voiced in the nineteen-sixties when certain activities were characterized and criticized as "ego-trips" by some of the very participants. Perhaps this suspicion of one's real motives, this introduction of self-doubt, is a response to some initial disappointment with a public cause that had initially caught people's enthusiasm. It makes emotional disentanglement possible without sorting out the difficult intellectual issues concerning the continued validity of this or that cause.

Once again, some asymmetries are to be noted here between private and public action. There is a considerable difference in the tolerance for mixed motives that is exhibited by the private and the public modes of action, depending on which is the primary or basic mode. Under modern conditions at least, the public mode does not tolerate *any* admixture of the private: probably because it is always under the suspicion of being *really* self-serving, the appearance of any explicit private objective in addition to the public one will serve to annihilate the credibility of the latter. In late 1940 the Marseilles owner of a small boat in which, for a substantial consideration, he was going to take political refugees, desperately anxious to leave France, to North Africa cynically explained his motives to me by saying: "I am doing this to save the honor of France and to make sure I am provided for in my old age." Here the alleged public motive could not and was not meant to be taken seriously: it was automatically and totally swallowed by the private one. But when a Colombian entrepreneur sets up a new sawmill in the tropical forest, fully expecting it to bring in handsome profits, he can exclaim "here we are building—forging—the fatherland" (*aquí hacemos—forjamos—patria*), *without* being considered ridiculous or hypo-

---

[7] By Paul Bénichou in *Morales du grand siècle* (Paris: Gallimard, 1948), p. 155. See also *Passions and Interests*, p. 11.

critical. In other words, a public motive and purpose can be credibly introduced as topping off a basically self-serving action, while the opposite operation is impossible. The claim to be doing good by doing well is acceptable and even plausible, whereas the inverse claim is not. Here lies another reason for the difficulties of a gradual and partial retreat from the public realm when, as a result of disappointment with it, there is a desire to reorient one's activities in the private direction.

Attractions of the Private Sphere

Until now the public-to-private transition has been primarily explained by factors originating in the public sphere. But the rapidity of the transition can also be explained by the strong attraction exercised by private pursuits after the first disappointments with the public life have been experienced.

The first of these *pull* factors has just been noted. It is the ability of the private life to tolerate an admixture of public motives. After some unsatisfactory experiences with the public life it is often possible for a person to stage a full-scale retreat toward the private life without feeling that he has become a renegade. He may indeed achieve the best of both worlds as he convinces himself that the public weal is best served by those who are strictly taking care of their own interests. We are all familiar with the powerful ideology that has this proposition as its cornerstone. The perspective developed here makes for the conjecture that this ideology served the essential function of *easing the transition* from public to private man. It assured those who had been brought up with the permanent injunction to serve the public weal, yet somehow found themselves absorbed by money-making activities, that they had by no means betrayed their calling. The extraordinary success of Adam Smith's doctrine of the Invisible Hand may owe much to the psychological needs of a certain generation of Englishmen, and indeed of Western Europeans, whose practice diverged sharply from the precepts which had been imparted to them. In other words, the idea that the public happiness is best served by everyone pursuing private gains may have served not so much a self-glorifying function for the new class of capitalists: it also fulfilled the more pressing need to relieve acute guilt feelings experienced by many a so-called "conquering bourgeois" who actually had long been exposed to a nonbourgeois moral code.

Moreover, once public man reels under the accusation of hypocrisy—the charge, that is, that public action is essentially self-serving—the turn to the private life can be viewed as a move toward reality, sincerity, and even humility. Just as the public life comes as a relief from the boredom of the private life, so does the latter provide a refuge from the paroxysm and futility of public endeavors. More generally, to be concerned only with looking after one's private needs, to "cultivate our garden," is to give up the twin illusory and hubris-laden pretenses of improving the world (*vita activa*) and of understanding its laws and secrets (*vita contemplativa*), and to attend instead to matters that have an immediate, down-to-earth usefulness and practicality.

But this humility posture is only one aspect of the triumph of private over public man. The ultimate ideological revanche of private over public action lies in the idea that the creation of wealth (the objective of private action) is fundamentally superior to the pursuit of power, which is now seen as the exclusive goal of public action. In contrast to the struggle for power, the creation of wealth is celebrated as a game at which all players can win. In particular, there are periods of rapid economic growth during which total concentration on private pursuits brings with it the satisfaction of participating in what promises to be a finally successful onslaught against many ancient scourges of mankind—and the feeling of excitement generated by participation in that movement can be as heady as the one experienced during a protest demonstration. Total immersion in the private life suddenly is felt as a liberating experience not only for oneself, but for all of society. The feeling is of course an important ingredient of The American Dream or Creed,[8] but it has seized other societies as well. Intellectuals

[8] David M. Potter, *People of Plenty* (Chicago: University of Chicago Press, 1954).

are usually not prone to extol this phase—they are repelled by its vulgarity, its neglect of the nobler pursuits (such as, precisely, politics), and its frequent disregard for social justice. But I have found at least one passage by a contemporary writer that catches this ideological moment remarkably well just because its attractiveness comes as a reluctant discovery:

> . . . when I went to Venezuela, I felt that for the first time I realized something about my own country which I had not previously seen there: the idealism which is inherent in what I had experienced [in the United States] as materialism and individual self-seeking. I saw that for Venezuelans, for whom economic development had just begun . . . the democratizing of material consumption and the opening up of opportunities—for those able to seize them—was a truly exciting and liberating idea.[9]

The only trouble is that our enthusiastic privatized citizen is now going to meet with the various disappointments which have been set out in the first sections of this essay.

[9] Lisa Peattie, "Cuban Notes," *Massachusetts Review* (Autumn 1969), 673–674.

CONCLUSION

With the return to private pursuits of the erstwhile public citizen I have come full circle. But some concluding comment is called for: one cannot just expose the foolish ways of human-kind in going through these gyrations and then quit. What, then, is the moral of my story? Not too deeply buried in it lies in fact a certain amount of moralizing. Before coming to that I would plead, however, that I have been intentionally far less moralistic than most previous writers on the subject. The many illustrious theologians and philosophers who have held forth on human conduct, starting with the dispute about the comparative merits of *vita activa* and *vita contemplativa*, generally did so with the aim of recommending one particular "life-style" as most pleasing to God, most desirable from the point of view of society, and most rewarding for oneself. It is just because I have refrained from fully endorsing any particular style that I have been able to concentrate on the movement from one to the other. I have tried to cultivate an empathy for both the weaknesses and the strengths of opposite styles and, as a result, my point of view has been shifting as my story moved along: first I marshaled the strongest argument I could find in favor of a turn to public action on the part of previously private-consumption-oriented citizens, and later I did the same for a turn in the opposite direction.

Now I have long believed that some pattern of change from one style to another is not only inevitable, but outright useful and desirable, that there is no *one best way*. Here I am in a small, but rather good company. Ecclesiastes pointed out that there is a *time* for planting and one for uprooting. There also is the related idea of stages through which life necessarily or ideally passes: Kierkegaard distinguished between the esthetic, ethical, and religious stages, and Hinduism had long laid down not too different a succession of stages or *āshramas* from student under the instruction of a *guru,* to active and worldly householder, to withdrawal from the world and finally total devotion to spiritual quest. The Hindu idea that it may be appropriate to adopt pointedly different life-styles at different times of our lives was endorsed by Erik Erikson in comparison with what he called "the almost vindictive monotony of Judeo-Christian strictures by which we gain or forfeit salvation by the formation of one consistently virtuous character almost from the cradle to the very grave."[1]

In addition to moving from one stage to another, individuals and groups have been noted to be subject to simple pendular movements. Some forty years ago, a fairly regular alternation between liberalism and conservatism—with each phase lasting from 15 to 20 years—was found to have been a distinctive *and* positive characteristic of American politics since Independence.[2] Similarly, some movement back and forth between the public and private life can be wholesome for individuals as well as for society as a whole. But such oscillations can obviously be overdone. That this is the case in our societies *is* the moralizing claim implicit in my story. Western societies appear to be condemned to long periods of privatization during which they live through an impoverishing "atrophy of public meanings," followed by spasmodic outbursts of "publicness" that are hardly likely to be constructive. What is to be done about this atrophy and subsequent spasm? How can we reintroduce more steady concern with public affairs as well as "genuine public celebrations" into our everyday lives?[3] How can we learn to take up public causes

---

[1] *Ghandi's Truth* (New York: Norton, 1969), p. 37.

[2] Arthur M. Schlesinger (Sr.), "Tides of American Politics," *Yale Review* 39 (Dec. 1939), 217–230. A revised version under the title "The Tides of National Politics" is in Schlesinger, *Paths to the Present* (New York: Macmillan, 1949), Chap. 4. Giving due credit to his father, Arthur M. Schlesinger has utilized this thesis about a political cycle in American politics in some of his more recent writings; see, for example, "Is Liberalism Dead?" *New York Times Magazine,* March 30, 1980, pp. 73ff.

[3] The words in quotes in this and the two preceding sentences are from Charles Taylor, *The Pattern of Politics* (Toronto: McClelland and Stewart, 1970), p. 123.

with enthusiasm, yet without the frenzy and the millenarian expectations that guarantee failure and massive disappointment?[4]

The divorce of the private and the public as a characteristic feature and a problem, even an affliction, of modern society is only one of several such splits. It has much in common, for example, with that between work and love, a dichotomy originally noted by Freud that has recently been surveyed by a group of social scientists and psychologists.[5] Industrial society has tended to empty work of affective and expressive elements and to make it into a purely instrumental relationship: you work in order to "make" an income—work is thus conceived purely as a cost incurred for the purpose of a wholly separate benefit. Love, on the other hand, stands in the dichotomy for the affective relationships that are ideally thought to be wholly expressive, that is, undertaken for their own sake with no thought of any utility beyond the one to be gotten out of the act of loving. Writing about the work-love polarity in Anglo-American society in these terms, a noted sociologist finds that "[t]his cultural opposition has dominated the structure of Western thought for centuries and has limited the number of moral and psychological solutions for the dilemmas of human existence."[6] Like the private-public split, the divorce between work and love is thus felt as impoverishing and stultifying. But as with all such basic polarities, it is easier to identify and criticize them than to come up with "constructive" proposals how to overcome them, that is, how to put Humpty Dumpty together again. Certainly, we can see elements that will be part of any such reconciliation. For example, a greater amount of workplace participation could contribute to healing both the instrumental-expressive and the public-private split: such participation would enhance work satisfaction—make work less purely instrumental—and

[4] A sensitive argument along these lines is in Glenn Tinder, *Community: Reflections on a Tragic Ideal* (Baton Rouge: Louisiana State University Press, 1980), Chap. 9.
[5] Neil J. Smelser and Erik Erikson, eds., *Themes of Work and Love in Adulthood* (Berkeley: University of California Press, 1980).
[6] Neil J. Smelser, *Themes*, p. 108.

would also introduce an element of publicness into the private work effort.

But this is not the place to draw up a blueprint for a society in which the private and the public realms would be less clearly demarcated and more easily inhabited together than is the case today. I feel that, in a way, I have already made a contribution to this task by accounting at length for the wide swings in benavior—from utter privatization to total absorption in public causes and back—that can be observed, or that I have constructed. To achieve a better understanding of pathological behavior means, to some extent at least, to bring it under control. This does not mean that more straightforward remedies are not indicated or could not be conceived. That task, however, belongs to a different discourse, and, fortunately, others have already placed it on their agenda.

But, rather than dwell on the limits of my inquiry, I shall point in closing to its potential. In accounting for the swings from the private-oriented to the public life and back again the notion of disappointment has provided me with a crucial mechanism. Disappointment implies some prior mistaken decision or choice, and my story is, in a sense, the unfolding of successive, rather large-scale mistakes with no assurance that a disappointment-free state will ever be reached. From this point of view, the story is not based on the "rational actor" of received economic theory, but on a far less accomplished character. On the other hand, I can claim just the opposite for the human types underlying my story: they are *superior* to the "rational actor" inasmuch as they can conceive of *various* states of happiness, are able to transcend one in order to achieve the other, and thus escape from the boredom of permanently operating on the basis of a single, stable set of preferences. Quite likely, these nobler and richer qualities of our actors are closely related to their bungling and blundering ways. To allow for such complexity was essential for my inquiry here; it may also be helpful, I suspect, in rendering other facets of social life and change more intelligible.

INDEX

addiction: and public action,
101–102
Addiss, Penny, 16n
Agulhon, Maurice, 113n
Akerlof, George, 42n
akrasia, 70
Almond, Gabriel A., 120n
Arendt, Hannah, 7n, 63, 83
Arrow, Kenneth J., 42n
automobiles, 16, 35–37, 38

Barry, Brian, 78n, 106n
baubles: *see* trinkets and baubles
Baudeau, Nicolas, 52
Baudelaire, Charles Pierre, 53
Baudrillard, Jean, 36n
Becker, Gary, 20n
Bell, Daniel, 39, 78
Bénichou, Paul, 127n
Berger, Marilyn, 87n
Blake, William, 19
boredom, 27, 57, 134
Brown, John, 50
Buchanan, Allen, 86n
Buddhism, 64
Burckhardt, Jacob, 126

Carlyle, Thomas, 122
chétives marchandises, 51, 53
cognitive dissonance theory,
15–17
colifichet, 50–51, 53, 54
collective action: *see* participation;
public action
collective behavior: changes in,
4–6
comfort, 27, 87; and durables,
32–35, 44
Constant, Benjamin, 7, 83, 97–98,
99

consumer goods: *see* durable
goods; nondurable goods
consumerism: recoil from, 50–
53
consumer services: *see* services
consumer sovereignty, 106–107
consumer surplus, 107
corruption, 123–25
cyclical theories, 4, 14–15, 132
Cyert, Richard M., 17n

Dahl, Robert A., 98n, 104n,
118n
Deffand, Madame la Marquise
du, 52, 57, 58
De Groot, Morris H., 17n
Diderot, Denis, 37n
disappointment: and expectations,
10–13; antonym of, 13;
importance of, 23–24; and
nondurable goods, 27–32; and
consumer services, 40, 44–45;
and newly expanded social
services, 42; and durables, 44;
and new material wealth, 46;
and shifts to political action,
63; exit-voice reactions and,
64–66; and private
consumption pursuits, 92; and
public pursuits, 92–93; and
participation, 95–96; and time
commitment, 96–97; and
corruption, 124–25; concluding
remarks on, 134
Dostoevsky, Fyodor M., 70n
durable goods, 32–38;
disappointment and, 18, 44;
subcategories, 34; finished and
unfinished, 37; and comfort, 44;
Adam Smith and, 49

Library of Congress Cataloging in Publication Data

Hirschman, Albert O.
    Shifting involvements.

    Includes bibliographical references and index.
    1. Self-interest.   2. Consumption (Economics)
3. Political participation.   4. Collective
behavior.   I. Title.
HB199.H49   330.1   81-47922
ISBN 0-691-94231-4   AACR2
ISBN O-691-00368-8 (pbk.)

Albert O. Hirschman is Professor of Social Science at the Institute
for Advanced Study in Princeton. His previous books are:

National Power and the Structure of Foreign Trade

The Strategy of Economic Development

Journeys Toward Progress

Development Projects Observed

Exit, Voice, and Loyalty

A Bias for Hope: Essays on Development and Latin America

The Passions and the Interests

Essays in Trespassing: Economics to Politics and Beyond